T0159115

LOSING SIX KIDS

My Failed Adoption Story

Losing Six Kids

My Failed Adoption Story

Christine Bonneur

Losing Six Kids
My Failed Adoption Story

This book is a work of nonfiction. It is an account of my experiences trying to adopt and living in Uganda. Because of sensitivity to family situations and the corruption within the process, some names and places have been changed and photographs omitted.

Holy Bible, New International Version®, NIV® Copyright ©1973, 1978, 1984, 2011 by Biblica, Inc.® Used by permission. All rights reserved worldwide.

iUniverse books may be ordered through booksellers or by contacting:

iUniverse
1663 Liberty Drive
Bloomington, IN 47403
www.iuniverse.com
1-800-Authors (1-800-288-4677)

ISBN: 978-1-5320-1451-2 (sc)
ISBN: 978-1-5320-1452-9 (e)

Library of Congress Control Number: 2017901621

Print information available on the last page.

iUniverse rev. date: 05/18/2017

ACKNOWLEDGEMENTS

Throughout the book, I mention so many wonderful people who had an impact on my life. But there are a few more I specifically want to thank.

Thank you to my grandfather. He's the greatest man I know. I thank him for loving me and supporting me through all times—the good and the bad. I thank him for being who he is.

To my sister, one of my best friends. Without her support, her friendship, her wisdom and her courage, I would not be much of a person. You make me better, Miriam, and I know I am so lucky you are my family. I don't have the right words to say all that you mean to me. But I'd be a raving lunatic without you.

I owe thanks to my parents. Dad, you have been so great, especially this last year after I returned from Africa. Thanks also to my mom who always loves me and has shown me what being a mother is. Thank you, Mom, for listening to me. That has meant so much.

To my brother, Stephen, and his wife, Copelia, who encouraged me and were so understanding, even when I missed their wedding by two hours. Thanks for Skyping and helping me see humor even in tough times.

To all of my family and friends here who loved and supported and encouraged me, and sent me e-mails when I was down. Thanks so much to Cindy, my mother-in-law, and Brian, my father-in-law, who always cheered me on and never gave up.

To Linda Marker, whose friendship, professionalism, encouragement and patience have made this book possible, and have made it better. I owe you so much and am blessed and humbled by your help and friendship.

Lastly, thank you to the people of Uganda, the Pearl of Africa—my Ugandan family and friends. You opened your hearts to me and I am grateful.

CONTENTS

PREFACE

I began writing this book almost immediately upon returning to Indiana. Even before leaving Uganda I had approached my good friend Linda, a retired editor, requesting her advice and help writing this book. I spent many hours in cafes, the break-room at work, or my dining room table writing, crying, remembering and processing all that had happened. Events and emotions that I could not openly speak about came easier to write about. I relied on memories, journals, e-mails and photos, as well as the plethora of documents I had from the entire adoption process. Everything is truthful and accurate to the best of my ability. Many names have been changed to protect the innocent.

Introduction: A Cautionary Tale

October 2015

Where does one begin to write when the words don't seem nearly big enough or real enough to hold the pain or the anger or the absolute feeling of being lost? It seems the place to begin is with the present, to explain what I'm feeling now, at this moment. Because, really, the past year —well, the past four-and-a-half years—have held so many moments.

Even though the process has ended, the moments are still there. The process ended without any conclusion, so the feelings and frustrations, the brief joys and the tormenting heartaches are etched in my mind. A movie reel of memories keeps replaying.

It was supposed to end with a triumphant return home. I pictured being greeted at the airport by friends and family with signs and balloons, hugs and tears, holding the hands of two little ones—our family.

But instead, I now feel that I'm being overly dramatic, feeling that I was denied something good. And I feel guilt for this sorrow.

Because I didn't lose what I never had. I lost a dream.

There are so many hardships in life, and I've "only" been disappointed. So I can't sit here and grieve like a martyr; I can't act like my world has shifted and changed, and I can't be a different person changed by a life experience. Instead, I have to shake off pity from friends, or impatience from family.

As I begin to write this, I have been home a little more than two weeks. Enough time to make a year in Africa feel like a dream, and enough time to realize that I don't belong anywhere.

I'm feeling empty and numb most of the day, which is preferred to the claustrophobia of anger that traps me at other times, making it hard to breathe. I want to explode and break everything and everyone in my path, but instead I'm trapped, holding it all in so tightly. No one sees me sobbing silently in the shower or holding it in until I can walk out of the room.

I know my family knows I'm hurting, but there are very few who *really* know. It's not their fault. I haven't talked about it. I can't talk about it. But I think everyone would feel happier if things just returned to "normal." Or whatever normal was before all of this.

Our home has two bedrooms full of clothes and toys and books. I've been collecting books to read to kids for years, because my favorite memory of childhood is my mom reading to my siblings and me before bedtime. Now I have to empty the rooms—sell or give away everything—because it's over. But every time I walk in the room and begin to pull things out, I break down.

How is it possible to hold so many memories of things that never existed? I'm beginning to feel crazy. Now I'm angry with myself. Why was I so foolish? Why did I think I'd meet my children? Why did I think my future held bedtimes and bath times and giggles and all those moments? Those were stupid, foolish moments in my head.

Instead, I have a house full of stuff and ghosts in my head, and I want it all gone. I don't want to be the person I was before; I don't want to pretend it never happened. I can't sit still while the world moves on.

I lost six kids in the span of eighteen months. And they were never really mine.

Chapter 1: "Children are the reward of life."
African Proverb

In a perfect world, there would be no need to adopt children. But because we live in a world that is broken because of death, disease, sin and poverty, vulnerable children are left in the wake. Ideally, those children should be in their own tribe, in their own clan, in their own home, and with their own families. When that isn't possible, adoption can create a new family.

I agree with the reasons for most adoptions, but I am strongly opposed to one. I do *not* believe that poverty is a valid reason for adoption. No family should have to give up their child because they cannot afford to raise him or her.

As a Christian, I believe we are accountable for recognizing this. If mothers or fathers are giving up a child for adoption because they cannot afford the child, isn't it our duty to help them keep their child? Because, if I take a mother's child simply because I was born into a privileged economy and am more financially able, then I am, in effect, stealing her child. I am telling her she is not worthy of being a parent. Furthermore, poverty invites corruption and thieves who come in the guise of "caring" agencies – and even social workers, pastors, criminals with sweet words of hope who paint a picture of saving children – when all the while they are breaking hearts and destroying families.

Sometimes as Christians in adoption, we tend to think we are doing a good thing; we might feel we are doing God's work, and then we overlook what is really going on. We must be accountable. We have to find the truth, and we must go into it with our eyes open.

I went naïvely into adoption.

I have learned so much—and yet I still don't fully understand. But I am now more aware of the corruption, of what adoption looks like, its ideals and its realities. Even so, I still believe there are so many children who need to be adopted to give them a family that every child deserves.

But not every adoption is ethical or what it seems. I now see that combining vulnerable children with a lucrative business called "adoption" breeds corruption. Therefore, we *must* be accountable.

I'm writing this book simply to tell my story of three failed adoptions. Yes, three. My story is full of anger and pain and frustration, but also full of redemption and reunification. It's a story of family and accountability. I'm not here to judge anyone else's adoption. I'm writing with the hope that my journey can help identify what accountability looks like when one is searching for the truth. Mostly, I'm writing because it's therapy, and it's the only way I know how to make sense of what happened.

Here is how my story began.

In 2003, at twenty-seven years old, I married a pilot in the United States Marine Corps. I've always loved adventure and something different. I have a degree in Aeronautical Technology from Purdue University in Indiana, and also earned my Airframe and Power Plant Mechanics license. I spent seven months on an internship with NASA in Safety and Mission Assurance at Kennedy Space Center.

I previously worked as a part-time zookeeper, taught school on a Navajo reservation, worked on an Arabian horse farm and a short-horn cattle farm. I'd waitressed, worked for cleaning companies, and worked for a fencing company in Pennsylvania, among other things.

So becoming the wife of a Marine and traveling across the country was another adventure. After seven months of marriage, in February 2004, my husband deployed to Iraq for almost seven months. He returned home in late September, unharmed and safe. But in late December, on Christmas leave at his parents' farm, he was in an accident while flying an ultralight aircraft. He sustained a spinal cord injury and a severe brain injury. He was temporarily paralyzed.

We spent six weeks in a hospital in Rockford, Illinois, then flew on a medical jet to a VA hospital in Richmond, Virginia. We were in the hospital a total of thirteen weeks, then another year of rehab where he had to learn to walk again. We spent the next few years recovering from the accident, figuring out what direction life would take.

In November 2007, he was medically retired from the Marine Corps, and we moved to Indiana, where he took a job first in Terre Haute, then a job in South Bend in July 2008 with a steel manufacturing company. By November 2008, the economy had crashed, with the steel industry taking a hit because of the collapse of the housing and automotive markets. He lost his job because of the economy, and thus began 2-1/2 years of being unemployed and searching for a job.

In the meantime, I took a job teaching preschool, and working for my mom's catering business. Once my husband was laid off, I took many other jobs as well, such as working for a cleaning company or stocking shelves at Dollar General. My husband took a temporary job with the Census Bureau, which also helped get us through financially. We decided to start a family, but because of consequences of his spinal cord injury, it became clear that we would not be able to have children of our own without medical intervention or another route.

After consulting with my doctor, I felt we were given certainty of success with adoption, whereas there was no certainty in fertility treatments. After thinking and praying about it, I felt certain that adoption was the right choice. I approached my husband in early 2011, telling him that I thought we should adopt. Initially, he was not interested in adoption. He wanted biological children—or none. I remember telling him that he needed to consider adoption and pray about it, because I wanted to be a mother and didn't want to resent not getting that chance.

In late February, he told me that he had prayed about it, and he felt that adoption was the right answer. I remember being extremely excited to start the process.

We talked about where to adopt from: a United States foster care program, private adoption, or international adoption. My husband was uncomfortable with foster care and the possibility of getting attached to a child who would never be ours. We had also heard of the hardships of foster care and didn't feel equipped to handle that. We looked into private adoptions, but also heard of the costs involved, with no guarantees, as the birth mother could choose another family or decide to keep the baby.

So I began to look into international adoption. There were so many agencies, and I had heard many successful adoption stories. Really, I was drawn to the adventure of it: traveling to a foreign country and being forever connected to that culture through my children.

Since 2006 we had sponsored three children through Child Fund International. One child, a young girl from Uganda, made a huge impact on my heart. She was born with HIV, which can be a death sentence in many parts of the world. With medication, she is able to live and go to school. Her spirit, determination, and her hope for the future, despite her illness, made me fall in love with Uganda.

A second reason I was connected to Uganda was because of my Uncle Gary's work with Scripture Union. He and my Bible study group leaders all attended a church connected to it. Scripture Union is an international, inter-denominational evangelical Christian movement founded in 1867. Its aim is to help children and young adults to know God.

In Uganda, there are many Bible clubs at schools and there is even a camp on Lake Victoria. One of the Scripture Union staff members was Beth, who came to the United States every so often on business. I met her a few times before ever going to Uganda.

My uncle had gone to Uganda to teach Scripture Union staff hermeneutics—understanding the meaning of the original texts or language of the Bible. He had also become involved in funding a chicken farm, which was located at their campsite on Lake Victoria. The hope is to earn enough money from their farm to sustain the camp.

Hearing my uncle's enthusiasm for Uganda and meeting Beth further increased my love for this small East African country. After praying about it, we decided to adopt from Uganda.

I had already been talking to my dear friend Holly who, with her husband, had adopted twins from Ethiopia. We talked about the cost and choosing an agency and many of the practicalities. One thing she had mentioned was that, if we wanted more than one child, we should consider adopting two at once to save cost.

Money may seem to be an insensitive topic to discuss when all adoptive families really want to think about is having a child, but the cost of home studies, paperwork, an agency and referrals—not to mention flights, staying in-country, medical expenses and more—all add up and can be astronomical. If couples adopt more than one child at a time, they pay many of the fees once; whereas, to adopt again in a few years means starting all over financially. In 2011 the cost to adopt two children from overseas was between $30,000 and $40,000. (To adopt one child was more than $25,000.)

Since my husband was still laid off, preparing to adopt would take a huge leap of faith!

I didn't know of anybody who had adopted from Uganda, so I began an online search. There were two agencies that seemed to have solid Christian principles. And one handled adoptions in Uganda! After contacting them online, we filled out an application.

From my journal:

February 26, 2011

> *This past Wednesday, our application to adopt from Uganda was accepted! Woohoo! So we are starting the journey. Our hope is that by this time next year we will have a boy and a girl, God willing. This is the coolest adventure. I'm so excited. I have lots of fears, make no mistake about that. But not only do we get to go to Africa, but we come home a family!*

> *Money. Money. Money. So I don't know where it'll come from for this. My husband is still looking for a job. Manna from heaven maybe. We've prayed about this and we feel it will work out if it's blessed. So far so good.*

> *So I may disappear under mounds of paperwork. The*
> *cool thought is our kids are out there, somewhere under the*
> *African stars. God bless them and keep them safe....*

After signing with an international adoption agency, we also had to find an agency to perform our home study required by the U.S. government. It determines if you are financially stable, if you are not criminals, if you are acceptable to be parents, if you have a house that is safe and large enough—and on and on!

There was only one agency in all of Northern Indiana that performed international adoption home studies. I called and we were promptly given an appointment for March 1 to have the social worker, Fran, come to our house for an inspection and to start the paperwork. The visit went well, and we were immediately approved to have children in our house.

We began telling all of our family about beginning the process to adopt two children from Uganda. Everyone was supportive and enthusiastic. My brother, Stephen, was so excited to have a nephew— mostly to be able to play together with cool toys. My mother-in-law was thrilled and promised to buy the beds. My co-worker bought me a photo album with brightly colored African animals on it. My mom, sister and grandfather, all of whom live nearby, were supportive from the beginning.

In mid-March, my husband had an interview with a company in Middlebury, Indiana, about 40 minutes from our house. Two hours after the interview, he was offered a job. We were so relieved and felt that this was confirmation of being on the right track with adopting. To get a job just weeks after starting the adoption process, when he had been laid off for more than 2-1/2 years, felt like God was blessing this decision.

From my journal:

> *Paperwork, Paperwork, Paperwork! That's what a*
> *home study is all about. And if your adoption process goes*
> *on for close to three years, you get even more paperwork,*
> *because you have to update your home study!*

> *We filled out state documents, county documents, national documents. We were fingerprinted multiple times and had many background checks. We had medical appointments and everything had to be notarized. We know more about background checks than I ever thought possible, and this is even after my husband was in the Marine Corps!*

> *But to tell you the truth, although it wasn't always easy and was very costly, there are parts of it that I enjoyed. I really enjoyed the extra trips and half-days that we spent together going to Michigan City, Indiana, to be fingerprinted and going to the police department to have background checks. So although I breathed such a sigh of relief that the home study part was finished, it was all worth it and it wasn't all bad!*

By mid-April, the home study papers and background checks were almost finished. I was in constant contact with our home study agent and the international agency agent assigned to us. But at that time, I was beginning to have some difficulties with the home study agent. She was constantly sick or unable to complete paperwork. We received many excuses, including illness, car accidents, computer crashes, cousin in a coma, and a daughter in the hospital.

At first I was sympathetic, but after about the third crisis, I realized that the delays were mostly excuses. Luckily, I felt that the great relationship with my international agents made up for dealing with the troublesome home study agent.

From my journal:

May 1, 2011

> *So I keep thinking about "our kids" somewhere out there in Africa. I believe God has you, our children,*

> *preparing us for you. We are moving, although slowly, on a path toward you.*
>
> *My desire is to have a family to share this life with, to expand in love and help me grow in faith and love and give me strength. I believe adoption has always appealed to me. I believe God is fulfilling my desire of a family in granting me this adoption.*

For the next few years of waiting, when I was up late at night, I stood in the backyard and looked at the stars, wondering if my children were under a similar night sky, looking at the same stars. I said many prayers. I felt more connected to my children, although I did not know them. I knew the same moon looked down on them, and I prayed they were safe and well.

In June, we drove to Michigan City to get fingerprinted by Homeland Security—the first of many times, as the process is good for only a year. Once the fingerprints were processed, we waited for our referral. Initially, we were told that the referral took three to four months, but as time went on, the timeline expanded.

In October, after e-mailing my international home study agent, asking about any news on a referral, I was told that the process was now taking approximately six months to receive a referral. But as time passed, it appeared that referral time in Uganda was more unpredictable than even our agency initially understood.

In February 2012, we were told that the referral waiting timeline was now about twelve months from being placed on the referral list. We had about another six months in that timeline and were hoping to get a referral by August 2012. Our agent felt that we would/should have a court date before December 2012.

One note about Uganda court dates: The family courts close for vacation from July 15 until August 15 and again from December 15 until January 15. Even after getting a referral, we knew it could be some time before we secured a court date, and if it fell around the court's vacation time, it could even be another month's wait.

Once we received a court date, my husband and I planned to fly to Entebbe, Uganda, which is about forty-five minutes away from Kampala, the capital city. Our agency suggested flying over only a couple of days before court. We would meet the children and, depending on the orphanage rules, they might be able to stay with us before court. After court, one spouse could leave Uganda and return home to work.

Our agency was now predicting that the other spouse would remain with the children in-country for approximately four to six weeks in order to get a court ruling, get the children's passports, medical checks and get through the U.S. Embassy and then return home. This was an approximate timeline that we found changed drastically over the next year.

One significant reason our timeline kept changing and becoming longer was because other African countries (such as Ethiopia and the Congo) closed their adoption programs (temporarily) because of corruption. Families wishing to adopt from Africa then chose Uganda, and their courts and the U.S. Embassy there became overwhelmed.

Corruption also brought adoption under closer scrutiny. Technically, to adopt in Uganda, adoptive parents must live in-country for three years. The alternative is called Legal Guardianship, which is granted to an adopting family by the Ugandan courts, with the understanding that the child(ren) will be legally adopted in the parents' home country.

We were informed in February 2012 that it might be difficult to adopt two children unless they were siblings, and we needed to consider adopting one, if two were not available. We agreed to this, but I was still praying for two. I was also told at this time about two new staff members—Laura, a Ugandan, who would help us get through court, and Kate, an American living in Uganda, who would help with travel and logistics when in-country.

During this waiting, I did what many expectant mothers do. I planned and readied the children's bedrooms as much as I could. I watched for sales and purchased a trundle bed that I put in one of our two spare bedrooms. Our agency had told us that in orphanages, the kids might be used to sleeping in a room with many children, and they might be afraid of sleeping alone. We had two rooms prepared to give them each their own space but, with a trundle bed, they could share a room for as long as they needed.

I bought a toy box and framed a few vintage travel posters from Africa for the walls. At estate sales I found dressers that I refinished as needed. The rooms began taking on life and holding all my dreams. A child's rocking chair held a few dolls, a bed was covered in oversized pillows and stuffed animals, and there was a bookcase full of books to read at bedtime. Without meeting my children, I still began to know them.

Our agency helped us prepare for adoption by suggesting websites and giving us a list of helpful books, the most well known being *The Connected Child* by Karyn Purvis, David Cross and Wendy Sunshine. Being a new mother has a learning curve for every woman, but to adopt one or two children out of traumatic circumstances and from a different culture has a different set of challenges to prepare for.

The book had advice on bonding with children, such as holding them, even if they were older, trying to create those mother-child bonds. There was advice on disciplining and how *not* to discipline adopted children; for example, any type of corporal punishment, such as spanking or even timeouts, is highly discouraged. Not knowing a child's history or past meant not knowing if he or she had been physically abused; therefore, any spanking could further damage a child's trust in a new parent.

I read as much as I could, trying to learn how to best parent my children-to-be. Our agency also had us view almost six hours of video information and instruction on how to parent adopted children.

I also wanted to learn as much as possible about the Ugandan culture and climate, its history and its people, the languages and food. I already knew I wanted my children to know and love their culture, and I wanted to retain ties with their home country. My husband and I had recently been informed that many Ugandan judges were granting Legal Guardianship with the stipulation of a "heritage trip."

This required the adopting parents to bring the Ugandan child back to Uganda every five years until he or she turned eighteen, in order to keep strong ties with their culture and country. I was excited by this prospect, even though I knew that it could be expensive. I had always wanted to visit Africa, and I was quickly falling in love with Uganda, this little country on Lake Victoria that Winston Churchill named "The Pearl of Africa."

In the meantime, our agency personnel were supposed to e-mail us regarding which number we were on the waiting list. By September 7, 2012, we were number three. Things had slowed down more than the agency had anticipated. I had my doubts at this point that we would be in court before 2013. They were still saying formally that it would only take twelve months to be matched with a child. At this point, we had been on the waiting list just over twelve months. By October, they extended the waiting to fifteen months.

We were beginning to have paperwork expire, such as our "biometric fingerprints" with Homeland Security, immigration approval, various background checks and local police checks. At least by this time, I knew some of the hoops and how to navigate them. Most of these updates had a one-time no-fee update but, after that, the costs began piling up again. We also had to update our home study since my husband now had a job and our financial situation had changed. This meant dealing with our home study agent who was becoming increasingly difficult to get in touch with and work with reliably.

It was at this point of the process that patience became a virtue. Trying to be patient was a challenge, because as time went on, we were moving backwards. Friends and family were also becoming impatient, and I fielded a lot of questions about why this was taking so long, or why I did not just change countries, because a friend got a baby from another country in two weeks. The other popular piece of advice was that we should adopt from America because there were so many babies here who needed homes, and we could have a baby next week. The comments were backed by kindness, and I appreciated the care, but I was getting worn out and feeling as if maybe this would never happen.

Chapter 2: Finally Good News: James and Kira

"For I know the plans I have for you," declares the Lord, "plans to prosper you and not to harm you, plans to give you hope and a future."
Jeremiah 29:11

Before the end of 2012, we were number two on the waiting list, hoping to be matched with a child soon. But by June 26, 2013, we were still number two. That changed, however, with one phone call on June 27. My agent called me with news of a brother and sister in an orphanage outside of Kampala, Uganda. The girl was four years old, named Kira, and James was nine.

Without going into details, we were told that because of an unusual circumstance from the parents' heritage, the children were outcasts. We were told that the mother gave the children up so that they would have a place to belong. They were both healthy. We were given a few sentences on their personalities from Laura, the Ugandan social worker.

> *James is open, friendly and talkative. He likes playing soldier and with cars. He likes art and drawing. He loves speaking English and English is his favorite subject at school. His favorite foods are rice, beef and chicken, but eats anything and is generally a healthy boy, according to his mother.*

Their mother also reports that Kira was too young to tell her personality, but her mother says that Kira likes to be loved and gets excited when they go to a supermarket. Her favorite foods are meat and rice, "like many Ugandan children."

I quickly had this information memorized, as it was all I knew about my children. We received three pictures: one color snapshot of each child, and an older black and white photo of them together.

They were beautiful.

From my journal:

On June 27, 2013, we first heard your names. Our American agent told us a little about you and asked us to think and pray over the weekend to see if this was the referral we wanted to accept. My dog Murphy and I were waiting for my husband on the front step when he got home from work to tell him the news.

I think it might have taken us less than thirty minutes to KNOW that you were the ones God had planned for us! The following Monday we received your pictures! They weren't even very recent or clear pictures, but I was in LOVE! It still took a few months, which felt like ages, before we got the full story on your situation.

We were finally able to sign the referral in late August. We received pictures of you and a video around the beginning of October. The referral is such an ominous thing. People wait months (and in our case more than two years) to find out who their children are. Once we signed, we wondered if you would like us, if we would screw up being parents, and how in the world do we get this right? But behind it all is a sense of peace and excitement.

> *This is the Bible verse I have focused on: "For I know the plans I have for you," declares the Lord, "plans to prosper you and not to harm you, plans to give you hope and a future" (Jeremiah 29:11). You are the prosperity, the treasure God has given us. We are blessed to be part of God's plan to give you Hope and a Future.*

We decided immediately to accept the referral and were soon signing more documents, paying final fees and finalizing our dossier. The dossier is all of the documents needed by court: the home study, background checks, referrals, biometrics, immigration approval, copies of passports, birth and marriage certificates, financial documents, etc. Everything had to be notarized and accurate.

We shipped the packet to our agency in September 2013.

We were informed that a group from our agency was going to Kampala for a ministry trip related to another program and would be at the orphanage our children were in. They could take a care package for us and then would send us pictures. I quickly put together two packages, each with a stuffed animal dog that resembled our real-life dog, a ball and Hot Wheels car for James, and a stack of plastic bracelets for Kira to share. In each bag, I also included a small album of pictures showing us and some of what our home and neighborhood looked like.

I didn't want to overwhelm them with a house or dog or anything too different from what they were used to. In early October, I received an e-mail stating that the orphanage director had given the children the packages. The director was thankful, but noted that the children did not fully understand yet.

As I write this, after living in Uganda for a year, I see the children's lack of understanding as a red flag. Almost all children in Uganda understand about going to America and, if they are truly orphans, they have a desire to be adopted and go to America. In my time in Uganda, I had children who had good families still ask me to adopt them and take them to America so they could go to a good school. James, now 10 years old, should have had a good understanding of being adopted. Why they "did not understand" would later become clear.

But at the time, the agency's e-mail that was full of pictures and even a video of our children, with James talking and both children smiling and laughing, was more than enough for me. I watched the video a hundred times. I couldn't believe how beautiful the children were.

After mailing our dossier, we were ready and just waiting on word of a court date. I was able to do some research about where to stay in-country. Our agency had a list of recommended places and estimates but, ultimately, it was up to us to find housing.

After searching and e-mailing different places, I found a guest house that had the best rates, and it was near the U.S. Embassy. The cost was $30 a day for adults and $10 for children. It included three meals a day, which most other places did not. Knowing that doing my own cooking in a foreign country would only add stress, I felt this was optimal. This guest house was owned by an American couple who mainly rented rooms to adopting families.

In the middle of waiting, checking my e-mail and phone messages twenty times a day for news or an update, my sister and mother were planning a wonderful adoption shower for me!

They decorated the basement/meeting room at church, and sent out adorable invitations my sister made, all in a vintage travel theme, complete with airplanes and an Indiana Jones vibe that I adored. They decorated with a globe and vintage suitcases and pictures of James and Kira. They also set up a laptop with a video of the kids that anyone could watch.

Mom made some traditional Ugandan and East African dishes and drinks, and had a game for people to match the dish with its name. We also had cards I'd made with envelopes asking everyone to write a little note to a boy or girl, telling them that they loved them. We planned to take these to the orphanage and pass them out to all the kids.

I had wanted to do this after hearing a man from Kenya talking about his life in an orphanage and how he once got a letter from a woman in England, telling him she loved him. He'd never had anyone say that they loved him, and it meant everything. I was touched by his story and thought of my kids in an orphanage, perhaps feeling abandoned and unloved. It was a neat experience to have friends and family come and pour their hearts into these love notes, connecting them with orphans on the other side of the world.

I was so humbled with the shower and the generosity and love given by so many. I received clothes and toys and gift cards, things to take to Africa, and things for the kids when they got home. I felt like I was going to be a mother, and so much love was already waiting for my children.

On November 1, we received an e-mail from our agency regarding court date possibilities. We were told that we might get court close to Christmas. In which case, we would be in Uganda for the holidays, or there was a possibility of a court date sooner with a different judge (Judge Noah). If so, we would need to be ready to travel at any moment.

But as time went on, we still didn't have a court date, and our agency said our lawyer in Uganda suggested we just fly over, and when the judge heard we were in-country, he might give us a court date. But if he didn't, we most likely would have to wait until January. This felt risky and expensive and, although we had waited so long, we decided it was best to wait longer. We had been told that if we waited to get our case heard by Judge Noah, who was very favorable toward Legal Guardianship, he would most likely rule favorably in our case.

The following is an e-mail I sent to my agency:

> We have been feeling the stress of not knowing in the last couple weeks, and waiting. I know we should never compare our process to anyone else's, but it has been challenging hearing that others received court dates, while we still don't know. But I feel much better after talking with you this morning. It seems like Judge Noah is the best judge to hear our case, and even if we wait a month longer, it is worth it to have Judge Noah.
>
> I feel a little conflicted in making a decision to wait but, really, it is still in God's hands. If the timing is best to go next week, there will be a date set and we will go next

week. If not, then hopefully we can secure a date close to Jan. 15th.

Have a great Thanksgiving,
Christine

So we continued waiting, but we were also receiving updates and e-mails from our agency concerning the general adoption climate in Uganda. There were more and more issues, and there were rumors about these issues continuing. Our December update from our agency included a paragraph about the ongoing debate in Uganda surrounding Legal Guardianship. The agency was receiving word that some judges were refusing to hear those cases at all, and that one judge demanded that the family live in Uganda for three years before they could take their child home. Some orphanages were beginning to refuse to place referrals for Legal Guardianship.

I remember being relieved, that even though our process was taking so long, at least we had our referral and just needed that court date.

On Friday, December 20, I received an e-mail from our agency stating that our lawyer felt we would have a court date in late January or early February. Our agent also said that, currently, families were staying in country for about nine weeks before the process was completed.

Getting this e-mail actually helped me to relax over the holidays. I was no longer on pins and needles waiting for a call to be ready to leave at any time before Christmas. I knew the holidays would help make the time fly and, although I was so excited to spend holidays with my little ones, I knew the holidays could be emotional and hectic. It would be better to have many months together adjusting and to celebrate Christmas 2014 together as a family!

I was getting very excited. I remember hitting the after-Christmas sales with my mom and sister, picking up ornaments and stockings and toys and clothes to put away for next Christmas. I carried an album in my purse with pictures of the kids that I'd received from my agency's two recent trips there. I was even pulling out the album and showing

Walmart employees the children's pictures. I was ready, I was in love with these kids, and I couldn't wait.

As the new year began, our current fingerprint paperwork was about to expire, so our agent wrote to the officer with Homeland Security assigned to our case and asked for an expedited appointment. We were able to overnight a check to Homeland Security and secure a date and time to get our fingerprints taken for the third time. By now we had the routine down perfectly.

In late January, we got the call that we had been waiting for. Our court date was February 18! We would leave Chicago on February 15 and arrive in Entebbe, Uganda, late on February 16. There we would be picked up by a driver and taken to our guest house, forty-five minutes away in Kampala.

Here is the e-mail confirming our guest house:

Dear Grace,

>*I had contacted you a couple of months ago about staying at the Guest House during our adoption process. We finally have a court date! My husband and I are looking to reserve a room for us and the two children we are adopting. We are hoping to reserve a room with its own bathroom. We are arriving on February 16, 2014, and my husband will be leaving on March 1. I will be staying with the two children until sometime in April. We are guessing at April 15 as a check-out date, but it could be sooner (or even later).*

>*Do you have a room that would be available for us starting on February 16?*

>*Thank you so much for the information.*

God Bless,
Christine Bonneur

Grace, a wonderful Ugandan lady who ran the guest house for the owners, Jack and Connie, responded with:

> *Hi, Good to hear from you. Yes we are waiting for you and we can't wait to meet you. Do you have a driver picking you up? Does he know our place? If not, he needs to come and see the place during the day. And also I need to give him the telephone number for the guard to call him to open the gate, instead of honking. Thank you very much and see you. God bless.*

Now we had firm plans and correspondence. It was real, and finally happening. I could hardly sit still.

On January 28, my agent asked me to fill out an application for a financial grant from ShowHope, which is a foundation begun by Steven Curtis Chapman. My agent felt we had a good chance of getting a grant, and any amount would be helpful. More paperwork!

That was really the last of our e-mail correspondence before our trip. Everything else was by phone call. We were given a list of contact numbers and an itinerary of our expected schedule once there. We knew we would be picked up by a driver and taken to the guest house on February 16, and the next day our Ugandan social worker, Laura, would come with a driver and take us to the orphanage to meet our children and take them back to the guest house.

We would go to court on Tuesday, February 18, and be heard by Judge Noah. My husband would return to the states on March 1. I would most likely be returning in April. That was the plan.

By a crazy coincidence, my Uncle Gary, Aunt Rose and cousin Jacob would be in Kampala the exact time we were there, and they would be on the return flight to the United States on March 1 with my husband. It was comforting to know I would have family with us. We made plans to catch up while we were there, and they could meet the kids!

Looking back now, I see that everything happened quickly. It was February and very cold here in the Midwest with snow. We drove the night before our flight to Naperville, Illinois, and stayed the night with my Aunt Terri and Uncle Bob. The next day we headed to Chicago's O'Hare Airport. It was my first time ever using a passport and flying internationally. I love airports, so I was looking forward to the trip and connecting in Amsterdam.

The flight to Amsterdam took about eight hours and, when we got there, we had a long layover. We were able to sleep on the airport benches, along with many other weary travelers. Even now, I remember so many details about that trip. Amsterdam has many connecting flights from Africa, and I watched one family from Africa with two little ones doing the same thing I was—trying to get some rest before the next flight. But the little ones were full of energy and happy to be off the cramped airplane.

I remember watching them, thinking about my return trip with my two children and wondering what that would be like. I was nervous, scared, and so excited and full of anticipation. I had packed some special books and toys with the return flight in mind. My mom had bought me a View-Master, one like I had as a child, where you put the round wheel in and look through the viewer to see a cartoon. Only the one I brought with me was updated, and it had sound! The reels were of dinosaurs and baby animals. They were just toys but, to me, they meant the return trip. They were special and were to be given on that long flight home.

We landed in Entebbe late Ugandan time – after 11 p.m. With jet lag and time differences, I had no clue what time it was. Uganda is eight hours ahead of Eastern Standard Time (in February). We got through Customs easily, following all the instructions our agency had advised us. We found a driver awaiting us at the gate. I don't remember our driver, or if he had a sign, how he recognized us or anything. But I do remember that drive!

I knew that Ugandans drive on the opposite side of the road from us, but the driving there is much more aggressive, and lanes are more like guidelines on the road. It was night and, where electricity was working, there were buildings lit up. But in many places outside Entebbe, people were using candles and lanterns to light their roadside stands. Night life in Uganda is very active, and many people sell food, used clothing, shoes and about anything you can think of on the side of the road.

There is music playing, and pollution from cars, trucks and burning trash gives much of the air a haze. I remember my first impression of Ugandan billboards, which are huge and vertical, as opposed to our smaller horizontal ones. But mostly, I remember being exhausted and afraid we were going to die in a car accident before even reaching Kampala.

We finally reached the guest house and were ushered in by the guard and, I believe, shown to our room by Jack, the owner. We were exhausted and, despite the noise of insects and nearby night clubs, we promptly fell asleep. The next morning, we had breakfast and waited for our ride to take us to the kids' orphanage.

The Guest House

Here is the account I wrote two weeks later at 2 a.m., which explains the heartache that followed.

This morning I sat in a church in Kampala, listening to the voices of a choir filling every corner of the building. As in many places here, it's kind of an outdoor building, almost a pavilion. There was a breeze running through and fans overhead keeping it comfortable. People here sing with all their heart; really, it's not singing, it's pure worship. How church should be. My mother-in-law had said to me recently, "When prayers go up, blessings come down." That's what was happening in this church. Songs of prayer were soaring up, thanking God for the blessings that were coming down.

Inside the bulletin was the story of the woodpecker. The story goes something like this: The woodpecker flew to the top of a tall pine tree and gave three pecks on the side. At the same instant, lightning struck the tree, shredding it, leaving it on the ground. The woodpecker thinks that he himself shredded the tree with his powerful pecks.

The point of the story is that we often attribute God's glory to ourselves. But instead, we must be like John, who said, "He must become greater and I must become less" (John 3:30). *I share this so that those of you reading this will know that my husband and I did nothing heroic or selfless here. We listened to God and He blessed us. He blessed us with prayer and support and amazing answers all packed into two weeks.*

Soon I will be leaving Kampala and sorting out all of this at home. But I want to write something before I leave, especially since we have gotten a lot of attention and prayers and even praise. The praise is hard to swallow.

For three years, we have been working to adopt. For the last nine months, we have been working to adopt James and

Kira. They have been a part of our household, our nightly prayers, pictures on the mantle, two bedrooms waiting for their coming. I carried their pictures in my purse and showed them to everyone, and I mean EVERYONE: the Post Office lady, the Walmart employee, basically anyone with a pulse who didn't punch me.

During all this time, we also prayed for the children's mother. We had been told that because of special circumstances, and we were assured it wasn't poverty, she had given them up for their safety.

Life, and every story, is always more complicated than we can imagine. We flew into Entebbe on Feb. 16ᵗʰ, and we met the kids Feb. 17ᵗʰ. We drove through Kampala to the orphanage, which was about a two-hour drive. We were in culture shock and jet-lagged, and we'd gone from 12 degree weather to HOT, which is what I believe the thermostat reads here, since no one can ever tell me the actual temperature.

Someday if you are reading this and are interested, I will tell you what Kampala is like, but that would take too long here. Needless to say, I LOVE it here. But my next trip will include an arsenal of bug spray. I digress.

From the minute we met the kids, Kira was in our laps, calling us "mom and dad." We found out the next day that this was <u>not</u> a good sign. James ran away from us. Translators said he was upset. He didn't even have a picture of his mom. We also learned that Kira was wearing a new dress her mom had recently bought her, and that the kids had gone home with her for three days during Christmas. This was surprising to us, as we had thought they had no contact with her since being in the orphanage.

We knew initial meetings were emotional and scary on both sides, so we were not too alarmed.

We spent about an hour at the orphanage and then took the kids with us to our guest house, stopping on the way to buy James shoes for court. The rest of the afternoon was spent getting to know them a little, but mostly my husband and I were staring at them in disbelief. We were probably acting like all new parents who bring their babies home for the first time—worried that they might break the kids or ruin their lives by using the wrong soap at bath time. Luckily, James is nine and Kira is four, so they aren't quite as breakable.

On the next day, we were supposed to go to court, but we had been told that they cancelled our court with one judge in favor of us going before another judge. We didn't have a court date, and we had just found this out. This was concerning, but we were occupied with getting to know the kids. Each day that week we expected to get a court date and, finally, we were told it would be Friday afternoon. The time between Tuesday and Friday was not what we had expected.

James and Kira are beautiful children. They played with the other kids at our guest house, a total of twelve, nine of whom were being adopted. Kira loves to laugh and smile and get attention. She loves to swing and follow me around everywhere. She loves to dance, and these kids here are born dancing; they put us to shame in the States. Every kid in the house had better moves than James Brown! Kira didn't speak much English, but she could get her point across, as most girls can.

James quickly became the favorite of everyone in the house. He was brotherly to the younger kids, sweet with the babies, intelligent, with a hilarious sense of humor. And the best was that he would listen to instruction and always try to do everything better. This was a son we would be proud of. We are proud of him. To have endured what he has at nine years old, yet behave like a man, is not something you see often. He was sensitive, but tough. He was the best.

So now here comes the story. Between Tuesday and Friday, despite how great these kids were, something was horribly wrong. I was sick, emotionally. These weren't our kids. I told my agent we were babysitting someone else's kids. I talked to other adopting parents in the house and they reassured me that we don't always attach immediately to our kids. It can take time.

I kept praying, but I felt lost and guilty. I had so much guilt that I made myself physically ill. If it had just been me, I would have thought it was fear driving all these emotions, and I did think that for most of the week. But my husband was feeling the same way. He was great, by the way. I see now the kind of dad he will be. He played with the kids, was patient with them, laughed with them – and he gently corrected them and encouraged them. It's always a blessing to find out your husband is also a great father. But, unfortunately, we did not feel like parents to these two kids. After nine months of anticipating this week, we were so lost. We prayed together each day, trying to figure out what God wanted us to do.

My aunt and uncle and cousin were also in Kampala doing mission work for Scripture Union. They had planned their trip a year ahead of time, and our first two weeks in

Kampala (of which we had thirty days' notice) coincided with their trip. Before we left, we had a night of prayer with our Bible study group, which included my aunt and uncle.

My uncle truly thought it was God's timing to have us there together, and that he would be able to encourage us if needed. At the time, I thought "We will be with our kids. Why will we need encouragement?" But looking back, we can see God's protection and blessings at every step.

We met with my family for dinner on Wednesday night with the kids. They knew things were not going well and they encouraged us and let us know they were praying for us. From then on, they kept in touch daily.

By Friday morning, my husband and I were ready for court. We were in a better place. We had prayed and prayed and we decided that if we went to court and the judge ruled in our favor, then the kids were meant to be ours. We would just need time to attach. But if the mother changed her mind or the judge ruled against us, then we would know why we felt the way we did.

We arrived at court with the kids and sat in the waiting room with Laura, our Ugandan case worker, and a young lady from the orphanage. She took the kids on a tour of the courthouse, which was helpful, especially since Kira thought we were in the jail.

We were waiting on the kids' mother to get there. It appeared that the mother had not told the kids what was happening. Laura had wanted her to do that before we went into court. In the meantime, we found out that the kids had <u>not</u> spent the last two years in the orphanage.

They had spent some of that time living with the orphanage director and his wife, calling them "mom and dad."

Throughout all this time, they still had contact with their mom. This is why Kira so readily called us "mom and dad." It didn't mean anything, except that we were new caretakers. She had a "mom," who, regardless of the title we shared, was her one and only mom.

After thirty minutes, the judge called us up, but our lawyer and the mother weren't there yet. The judge was annoyed, and sent us back down to the waiting room. Soon they arrived.

When the kids saw their mom, we knew. Their faces lit up. Kira was immediately in her lap, holding her hand. James was all smiles. This was the most awkward moment of our lives and was completely unsettling.

Our lawyer went up to the judge, but the judge was now mad at his being late and told us to leave and come back next Wednesday afternoon. Anyone who has adopted realizes that every day you don't have court costs more money, more time in-country, more time waiting on a ruling, and more stress.

But, looking back, we once again clearly see God's protection and blessing. If our lawyer had been on time, we would have had court, and perhaps not had the opportunity we did.

As we left court, and shared a ride with their mother (also surreal), we were informed by our case worker that on Monday my husband and I would go visit the children's mother at her home. At the time, I thought this was outrageous. We were uncomfortable enough already. How could this be a good thing?

I should explain a little about the circumstances. Without going into their private details, I can say that we were told that the children were given up for adoption NOT because of poverty, but because of a tribal taboo. We were told that the kids were put in an orphanage for their own safety. That they had no life in Uganda and their mother was an outcast as long as the kids were with her. None of the reasons has any bearing in the United States; Uganda has a different culture and there are many tribes here with their own subcultures.

Of course, we were now seeing a different picture, one where the children still had contact with a loving mother and were still able to stay at her home, with relatives, in safety.

So on Saturday, we went with the other adopting families in the house to a local pool. Sunday we went to the city of Jinja with my aunt and uncle. (This is where the source of the Nile is.) Both days my husband and I were miserable. Now we knew why we felt we were babysitting. These kids had a loving mother! Someone they saw even after being put in the orphanage. Someone who loved them but felt she was cursed and had to give them up.

Ride on the Nile

Water Birds on the Nile

On the two-hour drive back from Jinja, when the kids fell asleep in the van, my husband and I talked and prayed with my aunt and uncle. It was like a mobile prayer group. We knew that God had given us a window to talk to the mother on Monday. We knew that we had to share the

Gospel with her. My uncle, who is a retired pastor, helped walk us through the way to give our testimony.

The next day, we spent two hours talking with their mother. We shared with her how we are all cursed by sin. It is only through the death of Christ that we are redeemed and purified. He broke the curse, cast our sin away. She was free if she believed. She had a Luganda Bible and we went over Scriptures with her.[Luganda is the most common language spoken in Uganda.]

We shared how we knew she loved her children and they were blessings from God. She did not have to give them up if she believed that Christ had forgiven her and she was no longer cursed. We had prayed ahead of time that God would use us to talk to her, that His words would be spoken and not ours.

Let me assure you, I had nothing to do with the two hours of talking that came out of my mouth. I couldn't have spoken and shared with her and prayed with her the way we did without the Holy Spirit. By the time we left, she had decided she wanted to keep her children. Praise be to God, and only God.

Now in the midst of all this, we found out lots of information. There are things in the story that I don't need to share, but which have a lot of bearing on this adoption referral. Many things came to light that made it evident that we never should have had this referral; in fact, it most likely would not have made it past the judge or the U.S. Embassy exit interview.

We were learning that there is a lot of corruption worldwide in adoption. Adoption can quickly turn into the buying and selling of children. We thought we had carefully chosen an ethical, U.S. Christian agency, and I won't yet point fingers, but I do have this to say:

We were told that our agency saw adoption as a ministry, not just their business. They told us that the Ugandan lawyer they work with also sees it as a ministry. We were also told that the orphanage director was a strong Christian, and this was a ministry to him.

My question is: Who in all of this ministry was ministering to the mother? If she had given up her kids because she felt she was cursed, why did no one share the Gospel and MINISTER to her? If God hadn't protected my husband and me every step of the way, we would have missed this, and I believe we would have realized it too late. We would have been just as guilty as if we had stolen her children. It has opened our eyes to our accountability, not only in adopting, but also in going through life.

Even now things are not resolved.

God blessed us by putting in our path an organization here in Kampala that specializes in reuniting parents or family members with orphans. They set up grants for the mother and guide her toward self-sufficiency. They check in on the kids weekly. They send pictures back to us and let us know how they are doing.

All this is amazing and more confirmation from God that He was guiding us all along. These were not going to be our kids, but He used us to make sure they could be reunited with their mother, to make sure she knows she is also a precious child of God.

Now it would be great if this story had a happy ending. I truly hope it will. But we are finding opposition and roadblocks from our agency and from the orphanage director and lawyers here in the States. I hope that they are only temporarily dragging their feet, and that they will work to reunite these children. I hope that they do have a ministry, and that it wasn't a line we fell for. Because they <u>do not</u> make money on reuniting families. They <u>do</u> make money on adoptions. We shall soon see where their heart lies.

An important lesson I have learned is that, in many places in Scripture, God calls us to care for the fatherless. The most well-known scripture on adoption says this:

Religion that God our Father accepts as pure and faultless is this: to look after orphans and widows in their distress and to keep oneself from being polluted by the world. James 1:27.

Caring for the fatherless doesn't always mean adopting. Caring may mean reuniting children with their families. Adoption is a blessing and I fully believe God intends for all children to have families. But we must be accountable to finding out if they already have a family; otherwise, adoption becomes polluted by the greed and sin of the world.

Our agency says it could be months before James and Kira are reunited with their mother. If they work with this organization in Kampala, it would be only weeks. Our agency said it's very difficult to reunite families. The orphanage director says it almost always fails: the kids run away, they get beaten, they starve, the house is overcrowded, and on and on. God has handed the agency the solution; it's up to them to use it.

In the meantime, we had to drop James and Kira off at the orphanage director's home, after spending two weeks with them. Kira still had no idea what was going on, and she waved goodbye and went to play. I hope this means that her heart was protected in all of this, because she knows who her mother is.

But we broke James's heart—and ours along with it. He sat silently, but with tears rolling down his face. Even now, the pain of that is so overwhelming. We know we did the right thing, but the guilt remains. I hugged him so hard while James and I were both crying. He is only nine years old. I would give anything to make this right.

We have been shut out of the reunification process by our agency and lawyer here. They say we should not have sought outside help. We called them out on it, and now they assure us they will work with this organization, as they admittedly have no experience. They say they will contact them this midweek in order to get things rolling soon.

Although I have lost trust in our agency and lawyer, I plead with all of you reading this to pray pray pray each day for James, Kira and their mother, that they are back together soon. That the kids are not sitting in the orphanage for another six months. God has a plan here; we just need our sinful natures to get out of the way.

We don't know where it leaves us. My husband and I still love Uganda; we want to adopt. But we won't be moving forward with the same people. This is a loss of time and money. But we will continue to thank God for His amazing blessings and have faith that He has a plan for us.

I remember being in a tailspin. That two weeks was an emotional rollercoaster, trusting people then feeling like I was learning a whole new truth. When things were unfolding, I had been in contact with my agent and, at first, I thought there was a deficiency in me, not knowing how to be a mother. But as the two weeks progressed, I realized why I felt so unsettled.

The following e-mail tells how I explained it to my agent.

2/24/14

Hello there,

> *Boy are we gonna surprise you. So after we talked to you Friday after our attempt at court and meeting Roberta, James and Kira's mom, we were feeling low. We've been conflicted this whole time with heavy hearts, wondering what we were doing wrong, why we felt we were babysitting someone else's kids, why we didn't feel we were a family.*

> *Even knowing that attachment takes time, we felt such unrest. We still felt strongly that we hadn't made a mistake, that we had prayed about adoption and we felt like we were supposed to be here for Kira and James. So we were confused as to why we felt so laden with anxiety.*

> *So this weekend we continued with the same heavy hearts, praying and trying to figure out why we received no clarity. We even felt worse about going to meet their mother today (Monday). Well, Sunday we went to the city of Jinja with my aunt and uncle and, on the way there, we were driving in Kampala and, of all things, we passed*

the kids' mom's home. They were so excited when they saw it. I think that, looking back, we were able to see all the whispers from God, and what he was trying to do here. We are still amazed.

We began to think Sunday about talking to Roberta about the Gospel and the redemption through faith in Jesus Christ. We mentioned this Sunday night on the long drive, and my uncle had been praying for us all week. He began to encourage us. We talked and prayed on the van ride for two hours about listening to what God would have us say to Roberta.

Praise be to God.

Today when Laura came to pick us up, we told her we wanted to talk to Roberta—to share the Gospel, and how Roberta and the children are not cursed, how we are all forgiven through Christ. We had also made a plan after discussing with my uncle and then with Laura that after sharing the Gospel and praying with Roberta, we would let her know we will continue to be in James and Kira's lives.

Ok, I'm getting ahead of myself. We went, and for over two hours we talked and prayed, with Laura translating. We read some Scripture and mostly talked about Christ's redemption. Laura was wonderful, too. We talked to Roberta about her life and the turning point of choosing to live for Christ, knowing she has a hope and a future, even though it will not always be easy.

Well, we just prayed that God would speak through us, and it wasn't easy. But Roberta is a strong woman, and she wants to be an example for God. Can you imagine a woman saying she has been redeemed by Jesus, and she is not cursed, and her children are a blessing? Can you imagine the example she will be for her family, her clan and for James and Kira?

It's amazing.

We are going to have Roberta come to the house for dinner this week with us (we still have the kids for now) and have everyone in the house pray with her. One family that is here is a pastor and missionary family. So this is exciting.

My husband leaves Saturday. I will see if I have everything set up for Roberta by then, or I can stay another week or few days if necessary.

Again, Praise God! A family united, a family that will be a light for God's redemption.

Ok, we do admit the bittersweetness in that we are not going home with kids. But we are not giving up on adoption. Laura is telling all this to our attorney today; he doesn't know yet either.

Can you believe God sent two clueless people all the way from Indiana to Kampala to find a lost sheep and restore this family.

I know your office has been praying for us as well, so we thank you. Feel free to call.

Christine

Unfortunately, the joy of reuniting the kids with their mother was somewhat short-lived. At first my agent seemed positive, but then things got complicated. Laura, the Ugandan social worker, told our agency I had agreed we would buy the mother a new house and get her started in a business, along with supporting the kids in school. I called Laura back and told her we would not—and could not afford to— do all of that, but we would try to help the kids in school.

Then I received e-mails from my agent where it appeared we had offended Laura and she felt we were not honoring our promise. Furthermore, I began to get the impression that our agency did not see the situation the same as I did. Instead of believing that these children had a mother, and that I never had any right to be their mother, I felt our agency saw the situation as my deciding not to be their parent. Even now, I'm not really sure what their view of the situation was, partly because I never had a real picture myself.

My husband was on the flight out of Uganda with my aunt, uncle and cousin. But there were no other seats, so I had to wait another five days for a flight. I stayed with my Ugandan friend Beth from Scripture Union, who I had met in the United States at my uncle's house. By changing locations, my agency could not send anyone to harass me.

Beth lived in a two-bedroom house outside of Kampala. On Sunday, after attending church with her, we visited her sister at her house in Kampala. Beth told her sister the position I was in with the failed adoption. Her sister, Florence, was very sympathetic and kind. The following day, Florence called Beth and asked us to meet her on her lunch break. Florence had a job in the government. She had contacted a lawyer acquaintance of hers and asked him to meet us for lunch.

We met at a restaurant and sat outside under an umbrella. I remember having a lunch buffet and my first time trying matoke, a type of cooking banana that is common in East Africa. There are different ways to eat it, and it is a a staple in Uganda.

Thomas, the lawyer, seemed very sympathetic to my situation and we discussed the possibility of using him to complete an adoption in Uganda. He and his wife had adopted a boy years ago, and he seemed to understand the process. He assured me that he could get me a referral and court date in fewer than six months. He estimated the cost would be less than $12,000, in total, to adopt two children.

At the time, I thought this was fair, since we had paid so much more to our American agency. We exchanged contact information, and I left Uganda with the consolation that there was another opportunity. I felt this was a confirmation that God wanted me to continue and I would get my kids soon.

Chapter 3: Moving Forward: Benjamin and Anna

Not only so, but we also glory in our sufferings, because we know that suffering produces perseverance; perseverance, character; and character, hope. And hope does not put us to shame, because God's love has been poured out into our hearts through the Holy Spirit, who was given to us.
Romans 5:3-5

Once home, it was difficult to face not having James and Kira. I felt that I had experienced a loss – and still do. I had sewn blankets for their beds, hung pictures and art in their rooms, and picked out books and toys. There were framed pictures of them all over the house. It's hard to explain. They were never really my children, but I missed them as if they were. I was glad to be working with Thomas on a new adoption, but I was tired, I was cautious, I was heartbroken.

In the meantime, our American agency was trying to quickly do damage control. My agent e-mailed and asked to call and speak with us. I told her the times my husband would be at work. They called me in the afternoon while he was at work. I was on speaker phone with a number of people, including the agency's international director. It appeared to me that they were recording the conversation, and that they had consulted their legal department before talking with me.

The international director asked if he could pray over the phone before we talked. He prayed that the truth would be told. I was instantly angry. He then began the conversation by telling me they had "found" the blog I had written. This was interesting to me, as I had a blog called "Bonneur Adoption." I had two posts. One was a fundraiser, posting pictures of blankets I had made and was selling. The second post was what I had written in Uganda before leaving. In the post I never mentioned my agency by name.

They had purposely searched until they found this post. I now knew they were talking with me to ensure that I would not damage their reputation; they were, in effect, "dealing with me." The international director said he found and read my blog and that I was a very good writer. He asked if I would be interested in rewriting the blog so that they could publish it. I am still annoyed that he asked this. How could I rewrite it in order for them to publish, in order for them to look good? How do you rewrite the truth?

I was very aware, and his hints reminded me, that I had signed a "risk statement," stating they were not liable for things that happened in-country, as they had no control. It was clear to me that this phone call was a reminder that I could not say anything publicly to harm them.

I made it clear that I could not rewrite my blog posting. I continued to work with my agent and the group that was to get James and Kira back into the same house with their mother, and make sure that guardianship was restored to her. I received pictures throughout the process, and by May I received an e-mail full of pictures showing the mother going to the orphanage to pick the kids up and take them permanently to their new house. The smiles and expressions on their faces still bring tears of joy. God is good.

In the meantime, I received an envelope from Show Hope, the grant my agency had me apply for. We had been awarded a $5,000 grant. I immediately contacted Show Hope and explained that we had failed to adopt James and Kira and that the money should be given to another family. But after hearing our story and that I was working with a Ugandan lawyer, they said they would be glad to hold the grant for us until an adoption was completed. I was humbled and gratified by their kindness.

In May, my sister and I attended the Christian Alliance for Orphans (CAFO) summit near Chicago. It was our second year attending. This time was more difficult for me. During the two-day conference, I received an e-mail from Jacob, an assistant lawyer working with Thomas on my adoption referral. In the e-mail was information about a referral with the name of Pastor Mark, from a Pentecostal church. This pastor had a large church following and was taking care of the mother and her baby and young son. The e-mail also said that the mother was going to abort the baby, but the pastor convinced her to have the baby and was helping her pay her medical bills and care for the mother and children.

He sent me information and pictures of children, including one of a two-week-old baby girl. In the picture, the baby was being breastfed by her mother. I was appalled. I had thought Thomas understood my situation and my strong feelings, that I would NOT be taking any children away from a mother. I wrote the following e-mail immediately to Thomas.

May 5, 2014
Hello, Thomas,

> *First of all, thank you for your hard work and sending us this information. The pictures are beautiful, absolutely beautiful. My heart breaks for that poor mother and what she has gone through and is going through.*
>
> *If I understand correctly, the children are living with their mother, and not in an orphanage. It is wonderful that she is taking care of them and that the church has been so supportive of her.*
>
> *As far as we are concerned, although I would desperately love to adopt these children, I do not think we can.*
> * *I feel we would be perpetuating the myth that Americans make better parents because they are wealthier. This mother is obviously a hard worker, the children are living with her, they look healthy, and she must love them very much. I realize that*

financially we are so much better off, but poverty does not make for poor parents.

- *I do not think the U.S. Embassy would allow us to adopt these children. We have friends we met in Kampala who were adopting at the same time as we were in February, and they have all been denied visas for the children at the U.S. Embassy exit interviews because the children had existing family. The only case we know that went through was one family in which the boy they were adopting had been abandoned and no family could be found.*

- *After what we went through in February, and after having been told that the mother wanted to give up the children for a better life, we met the mother and found this to be not true. She did want the best for them, and she did want a better life, but she loved her children and did not want to give them up.*

I wish so much that I had a different answer but, from this information, I don't think we could adopt these children.

Do you have more insight or information on this case that differs? I would really like to hear your advice and thoughts as well. I will be praying about this all day, but I wanted to reply as soon as possible.

Thank you so much
Christine

On May 12, 2014, I received a new e-mail from my lawyer, with a possible referral. It contained information about two children whose parents were deceased, and the children's only living relative was an aunt.

Hullo Christine,
Greetings.

> *Please receive herewith pictures of total orphans Anna (Female) and Benjamin (Male). Stated to have been born to NGASIRWE JOHN and FLAVIA RUTIRINGIRWA, both deceased of KYARANGA VILLAGE, RUKOKI, KASESE DISTRICT, UGANDA on 4ᵗʰ April 2009 and 7ᵗʰ July 2010, respectively.*

> *Both children are under the temporary care of CHRISTIAN HEALING MINISTRIES based in the District of Kasese, Uganda.*

> *Kindly instruct us on the way forward.*

Regards,
Thomas

Along with this e-mail, we received a picture of a young boy and girl standing with a man. We asked for more information as soon as possible.

Here is the e-mail exchange from May 19, 2014.

Dear Thomas,

> *Thank you for this information. Are there health records or information on the children? Does Pastor Mark run an orphanage out of the church? Is this where the children have been living? How long did they live with their aunt?*

I am very sorry that their parents are deceased, but this is the kind of referral we want. I think we have a better chance of completing an adoption with this referral.

They are beautiful children.

Thank you,
Christine Bonneur

5/22/2014

Hullo Christine,

We have verified the following facts:
- *The children stayed with their aunt from 2011 to 2013.*
- *The children were placed in a church-rented house with other needy children in 2014. However, the facility is not an orphanage, but a home rented for the charitable purpose of keeping such needy children.*
- *The children have been fully immunized. No serious health problems are on record based on this information. I hope we may move forward.*

Best regards,
Thomas

5/22/2014

Thank you, Thomas,

Yes, please move forward.

Christine Bonneur

5/23/2014

Hullo Christine,

Thanks for the last mail.

In order to move forward, we need updated copies of all the documents you earlier mailed to us, including copy of notarized Home Study whose time has since expired. Later, as you come for the adoption proceeding, please bring along hard notarized copies of all the required documents. Further, we will need at least an additional sum of U.S. $5,000 to enable us to swiftly move the process.

Best regards,
Thomas

5/25/2014

Hello Thomas,

I've attached our current home study, which should still be good, although our immigration approval does expire July 27th. We are currently working to update our home study. Unfortunately, our home study agent quit her business and just informed us with no warning. We have found a new agency to update our home study and they say they will have it done within four weeks. They said if we pay them extra, they can expedite the process. I believe they could then have it updated in maybe two weeks or so.

Would you want us to have them expedite the update to get it done sooner than four weeks? If that is necessary, we will do so. If you can proceed while they are doing the home study update, that would be great. Just let us know how soon you need it done and we will do our best.

> *I will be glad to wire you the $5,000. Should I send*
> *it by Western Union again to the same account as before?*

Thank you,
Christine Bonneur

This was a stressful time—trying to update the home study, keep our immigration approval current, paying extra unexpected fees. We were also dealing with policy changes from Homeland Security regarding international adoption laws. They were no longer allowing independent international adoptions, meaning adopting without using a certified American agency. They were also requiring agencies to be Hague Accredited, which is the common international certification.

But it appeared there was a loophole, in that those in the adoption process and who had their immigration approval prior to July 2013 would be "grandfathered" into the system and allowed to continue even without using an agency. I had to consult my previous agent and a local lawyer to be certain. The lawyer said we were fine, and the agent counseled us against proceeding but, as I had no trust in their counsel, we went on.

We did have to do another home study update and, at this time (as I had mentioned in my e-mail to Thomas), our home study agent, who had been so unreliable, now told us she quit. This was cause for panic, as there were no other international home study agencies in our area, and we would have to travel a few hours to the nearest one. Furthermore, it could cost thousands of dollars to start over again! Luckily, I found another agency that was so kind to work with us and the home study we already had done. They updated it without starting from scratch, and charged us a much lower fee, while also having it done very quickly.

During this time, I was trying to prepare the house for two children who were much different in age from James and Kira. Benjamin had just turned four, so I was going to garage sales trying to find fall and winter clothes for him. Anna was said to be five but, from her pictures, she looked tall and so much older. When she stood next to Benjamin, there was a huge difference in height.

I e-mailed Jacob (assistant legal worker with Thomas) and mentioned this and asked what size she was. He assured me she was only five and that he would ask the pastor to take her measurements. I was hoping to bring some clothes with me that they could wear at the guest house, and also a nice outfit they could wear to court. It is not unusual for incorrect ages of children to be given to potential parents. Many Ugandans do not have birth certificates and, during the adoption process, the lawyers have the birth certificates made.

Furthermore, because adoption is such a lucrative business, children are often said to be a younger age than they are. We were approved by Homeland Security for age five and under. I knew that it was very likely that Anna could be a little older, but was listed younger just so she would fit into our profile. We had gotten an amendment to our approval for James since he was 10 but, this time, they still insisted that Anna was five. I assumed we could sort it all out later.

By June we were ready to mail our affidavit to Thomas. We exchanged the following correspondence.

6/18/14

Hello Thomas,

> *I mailed the affidavits yesterday using FedEx. It is supposed to reach you by next Tuesday. Please let me know if everything is in order.*

> *I was also informed that our new home study is in the mail to me. I should receive it tomorrow or Friday. I will e-mail you a copy, and I will send in our immigration update request ASAP.*

Thank you,
Christine Bonneur

6/19/14

Hello Christine,

Thanks for your last mail. We will receive the money after 58 hours from the date of deposit, and confirm. Since you will be in Kampala for a greater part of your stay, we suggest that you book in the guest house where you last stayed.

Meanwhile we will ensure minimum in-country expenses through our known contacts. We will also meet expenses for processing the children's passports.

Be assured of our unfailing support.
Thomas

By this time, I was feeling like things were under control. We were accomplishing everything in time, and I was sure Thomas was a blessing. Soon I would be meeting my children! I had felt that James and Kira were not supposed to have been mine. Instead, I was in that place and time with them in order to reunite them with their mother. There was a reason it happened and this did not alleviate the heartache, but helped make it easier to bear. I could look forward soon to getting acquainted with Benjamin and Anna, and I was beginning again to visualize what my family would be.

Our lawyer, Thomas, in Uganda now handed over our adoption process to his junior lawyer, Jacob. Then Jacob began to collect all the paperwork, including investigations, supporting documents and interviews that Uganda requires in order to go to court.

On July 18, 2014, I received the following e-mail.

Hello Christine,

It has been long. We have been doing our best to ensure that your matter is finally fixed. We have encountered some challenges but we are hoping to have the court date soon.

We had prepared to file your application in Fort Portal however we found out that the judge there wasn't willing to let you travel with the children from Uganda until you have stayed here for 36 months which cannot be possible on your side.

We managed to change the place for filing the application to Kampala where we hope to succeed with a guardianship order allowing you to emigrate with the children to USA.

Benjamin celebrated his birthday on 7th July.

We are likely to get the court date hopefully before the end of next week. A challenge we are facing is that courts here are on vacation until 15th August. So the date is likely to be 15th August and above.

You will need to notarize all the documents that were attached on the affidavits you sent. Each copy should be notarized.

About the photos and video clip of your children I managed to take some and copies are hereto attached.

With regard to passports for the children we are likely to get them within one week from today.

The children are in school but the pastor taking care of them is anxiously waiting for you to take care of the children.

I also met their aunt Ms. Leah and she is also delighted about the process. She signed some affidavits as well.

About the place for staying when you come to Kampala, we think you will use the place you had stayed in before.

We will keep you posted once we have the court date.

Jacob
Advocate

I received six photos with the e-mail, all taken by Jacob with his phone. Four were of the two kids alone, in school uniform. One was a picture of the kids, the pastor and their Aunt Leah, and the last was a picture of the kids and the pastor in his office, it appeared.

During all this time, I was wiring money via Western Union, in installments, to pay Thomas.

Finally, in August we received the news I had been waiting for!

8/6/2014

We are glad to inform you that the date when your application for guardianship will be heard has been set on Thursday 2nd of October 2014 at 9:00am at High Court Family Division in Kampala.

Kind regards
Jacob
Advocate

8/6/2014
Hello,

When we look at buying plane tickets, how many days ahead do you recommend we arrive before the court date? My husband can really only miss work for about a week (five working days).

Do we need to travel to Kasese to meet the children and bring them to Kampala? If so, how many days should we plan for that?

Thank you,
Christine

8/6/2014

We suggest you arrive on 27th-28th September which is a weekend, we can travel to Kasese and get the children on Monday 29th September, have Court on Thursday 2nd October, then your husband may travel back on Saturday 4th October 2014.

Confirm to me if this Schedule is okay with you.

Another good news is that we have already processed their passports through Pastor Mark and they are in my possession.

Kind Regards

JACOB
ADVOCATE

I e-mailed Grace at the guest house. We had been in touch ever since I'd received Benjamin and Anna's referral. Now I could make firm plans for coming back!

I purchased tickets on Delta Airlines, and we were scheduled to leave Chicago's O'Hare Airport at 4:10 p.m. on September 27. My husband would leave Uganda on October 4 and arrive in Chicago on October 5. I hoped to return some time in November with the children. My secret wish was to be back in time for Thanksgiving, but I knew that things come up, and I could not be sure how quickly the process would go. I was hopeful, though, as Thomas had already retrieved the children's passports, which was a surprise, too. With our American agency, I understood that we would have to apply for the children's passports after getting the guardianship approval from the Ugandan courts. But Thomas had already gotten their passports and was assuring me that the process would move quickly.

September came and went quickly. Before long it was the 27th, and my mom and sister were driving us to the airport. This time I felt more confident; I knew what to expect. I looked forward to seeing Jack and Connie and Grace and all the friends I'd made at the guest house. I knew I might not bond with the kids right away, and I knew to let my heart grow to love them. This time I was calm, but nervous. I didn't have an agency to call and question, and I didn't have a safety net to walk me through the process. But I was thankful for my lawyer. So far he and Jacob had seemed very helpful and would walk us through the process quickly.

The plan was that Monday the 29th we would travel to Kasese to get the children, stay overnight, and return to Kampala on September 30. We would have October 1 to get to know the kids and prepare for court which was the next day, October 2.

Once we arrived, our friend Henry drove us, along with Jacob, to Kasese, which was about a seven-hour drive. Henry picked us up late morning, and we headed into Kampala to pick Jacob up in town. We began our hot, dusty drive to Kasese. Personally, I think the drive should be a lot shorter than seven hours, except that Ugandans LOVE speed bumps. I felt like half the journey was slowing to drive over speed bumps, especially around Fort Portal.

Riding in a car in Uganda, and in much of Africa, I suspect, can really wear you out if you are American. It's hot, normally with no air-conditioned vehicles. It's a lot of stop and go, lots of traffic in towns, with pollution and noise. But I love seeing Uganda and the countryside. The area of Kasese is on the border of the Democratic Republic of the Congo, in the mountains. Although Kasese is not much farther south than Kampala, it feels much warmer there. Because the city is at the foot of the mountains, the space felt much more open, with less forest and bigger skies. I remember trying to get video with my camera so that my kids would have a reminder of where they came from.

We arrived at Pastor Mark's church in early evening. In Uganda, it gets dark around 7 p.m. almost every night, all year-round. We arrived with about an hour or so of daylight left. The church was in the middle of a neighborhood of houses. There weren't really roads. It was bumpy, and we found a parking place behind a house.

The church was a large empty structure, with a cement platform foundation at the front. The windows had no glass, but iron bars. I remember feeling it was a lot of concrete, very hollow. The pastor had some plastic chairs brought out. Soon many women began arriving and sat on the chairs with us, and about eight to ten kids arrived. I had assumed we would meet the children right away but, instead, the pastor wanted to talk with us first.

He spoke English and, even now, I remember feeling that he spoke very forcefully. He spoke with authority, telling us how things were and would be; he was not hesitant or questioning. He explained how his parishioners were building the church. They were obviously very poor, as we could see by the conditions of the neighborhood and by the women in front of us.

The pastor explained that his parishioners were so poor that they had been building the church for twelve years, and the people gave all they could; but it was never enough. "We are family now" became his slogan for the next hour. He proceeded to explain how it would be our job to go back to our home church and raise funds. Furthermore, he emphasized that Anna and Benjamin would return to Uganda after getting an education in America and support their aunt.

Pastor Mark informed us he would be making a trip to New Jersey in the next year, and we would have to pay for his flight to Indiana where he would stay with us, come to our church and speak to the congregation about supporting him. He also wanted assurance that we would call him and the aunt regularly so the kids could talk with them.

This was such a huge difference from our last meeting with James and Kira. We were with this pastor close to an hour before we even met the kids! When they finally came forward (someone must have given them the signal that it was time), they appeared among other kids. I could pick them out from their pictures and nervously gave them hugs.

Off and on this entire time, the pastor was speaking to Jacob in the language called Otoro. Later, my driver and friend Henry told me the way they spoke to each other made it clear they were familiar with each other and seemed to be friends—at least more than acquaintances.

After meeting the kids, the pastor brought the aunt forward for us to meet. I remember thinking she was so thin and very frail looking. She wore a traditional red dress with large yellow birds on it. She seemed so unhappy, and she didn't smile. She spoke no English at all, and everything had to be translated. We had been told she had two children of her own, and the smallest one, about two years of age, was with her now.

We didn't spend long with her before Jacob and the pastor decided we had better check into a hotel before dark. Then we would come back and finish talking with Aunt Leah. As we piled into the van, we saw Leah standing there totally distraught, throwing her hands in the air. Something felt so sad about this situation. I was nervous and overwhelmed and exhausted.

Even in the van ride to the hotel and while checking in, the pastor was still talking to me, telling me how I could raise money for his church. His personality was abrasive. But I find that any time I am in a different culture and dealing with adoption, the feelings of loss and poverty are present. Here was an aunt who would miss her niece and nephew, and children who would miss their home and familiarity. It is a challenge to navigate or know how to feel or how to assess the situation.

A year later, after discussing all of this trip with Henry, he said,

"Something which I noticed was that whenever Jacob spoke to the pastor, he switched to their local language. I don't know why. The people around the church were saying bye-bye to the children, and it looked like we were taking them to Kampala for study, not America or for adoption, and that is why Jacob kept talking to the boy in their language. The boy was, I think, missing the relatives. But something I really noticed, which opened my eyes, was the gap that Jacob was creating between you guys and the pastor and the community members. He would not allow them to talk to you guys. At some point at night, the pastor was trying to ask something from you guys and Jacob told him in their language, 'Pastor I will see you tomorrow and talk about that. Don't ask them.'"

Even though I was so tired and would have gladly eaten dinner and stayed in the hotel room getting to know the kids, we had to pile back into the van and head back to the church to talk more with the aunt. By this time, it was dark, and we went into the church and sat in the plastic chairs that had been moved to the cement stage at the front of the church. Leah, the aunt, was so visibly angry and upset that Jacob took her outside the church and talked with her for about forty-five minutes before coming back in and sitting with us for pictures.

By this time, I'd had my fill of listening to the pastor's plans for fundraising. I had jet-lag and I was exhausted. After an uncomfortable amount of time, we finally went back to the hotel, promising to stop and see the pastor in the morning before leaving. I remember I gave the kids a quick bath and we had mattresses on the floor for them. There was a TV in the room with two news channels, and the kids were fascinated, as they had never seen TV before. We waited a long time for room service to deliver chicken and rice. I checked with Jacob and Henry to make certain they were okay with their room. I think I was finally in bed by midnight.

The next morning, we got ready and had breakfast in the hotel restaurant, which was very nice. It's awkward becoming an instant mom, getting kids dressed and fed breakfast when you don't even speak a common language. I was so thankful for Jacob and Henry, who could communicate with the kids. We were waiting to hear from the pastor.

We wanted to get going, because Kasese is close to Queen Elizabeth National Park.

In reality, one could spend a week there taking safaris, but we hoped for a two-hour drive through some of the park to see some animals. I was so excited! As it turns out, the pastor got busy and didn't have much time. He met us on a boda, a motorcycle for hire, on the side of the road—and that was it. I don't really remember what he and Jacob were discussing. I know I had to give money for the pastor and aunt to travel to court later in the week and for their hotel stay. Whatever it was at the time, I was thankful that the meeting didn't last long and we were off on our next adventure.

We arrived at Queen Elizabeth National Park mid-morning. We had the option of driving one of two routes through the park: a long route in which we would see lions and zebras and other large game, but that would take all day, or a shorter route that would only be a few hours, and where we might be able to see an elephant. They warned us, though, that since it was mid-morning already and the day was heating up, we might not see much of anything. So because we still had a long drive ahead back to Kampala, we opted for the shorter route.

I sat in front with the camera, next to Henry. We saw many different kinds of antelope, warthogs, and water buffalo. But I was truly so excited when we saw an elephant! We saw three during the drive. Anyone who has seen an elephant in the wild can tell you the thrill is amazing. It was a feeling of being connected to a world so big, so much greater than myself. I was as excited as the kids sitting in the seat behind me. They had grown up near here, but never had the chance to see such animals before. I have a picture of Benjamin giving me a thumbs up, the universal sign of enjoyment!

Elephant in Queen Elizabeth National Park

Waterbuck in Queen Elizabeth National Park

Queen Elizabeth National Park is at the foot of the Rwenzori Mountains. There are wide open spaces where you can see for miles. You can also get lost in the scrub and trees, driving across rugged dirt roads, up and down small hills, rounding every corner In anticipation as you never know which animal will be waiting. Although we didn't drive to any of the lakes, they are the reason such a variety of animals reside in the area. Seeing Cape Buffalo cooling in midday heat in a mud puddle was a joy! All the elephants we saw were taking advantage of the shade of small scrub trees, where they were also eating whatever plants were available. The air was filled with the chatter and noise of birds. Trees were covered with the nests of Weaver birds, bright yellow birds that create hanging nests out of grasses, plant fibers and twigs.

It was my first taste of an African adventure in the wild, and I was loving every minute. But soon we were were back on the road and heading toward Kampala. We got settled back at our guest house soon after dark. We were exhausted, but just beginning our journey of parenting.

Court was scheduled for Thursday morning. On Wednesday, Jacob called me and asked me to come to his office to meet the aunt. He said she was upset and just needed some reassurance that I would take good care of the kids, and I would keep her informed about how they were doing. This made me uneasy, as it appeared she was not comfortable allowing them to be adopted. But Jacob convinced me she just needed some comforting and was truly happy for the adoption to proceed.

I met him that afternoon, and Leah was there in the office. I tried to confidently reassure her that I would do my best to care for them, would love them as my own, and we would keep her informed about how they were doing. Everything I said had to be translated through Jacob. I don't remember her saying much or asking any questions. I only remember being nervous and trying to appear confident, although, in reality, I was anything but confident. I also remember how awkward the situation was and how, for some reason, I felt guilty.

I had made it clear that we would not take away someone's children because of poverty, and we had been told that this was in no way the situation. Thomas and Jacob had assured me this case was clear: two orphans who needed a mother and father. They had an aunt who could barely care for her own two children and wanted her niece and nephew to be adopted. So why did I feel guilty? After the failure of adopting James and Kira, I knew my emotions were mixed and confused. I knew not to trust how I felt, but simply to trust that things would fall into place.

I still felt that it was such a blessing, after the betrayal of our American agency, to have been connected with Thomas. I had been so clear this time on only adopting true orphans. I had the death certificates for the children's parents. These were clearly meant to be my children.

In an e-mail I sent home, this was my first few days' impression of the children.

This trip is so different, and these two children are completely different. I still hesitate to write too much, as we are getting to know them and their personalities. I think we may be a little guarded, at least until after court, and seeing if things progress well.

But I will tell you a little. They are definitely brother and sister! They hold hands and help each other and look after each other so sweetly. But they also fight like cats and dogs. This cracks me up, because, although I don't understand a word they are saying, I KNOW I've said the same thing to my brother and sister at that age.

So we are working on a few things. Sharing is one, and not peeing outside and anywhere is the other. Bathrooms are a newer concept, I think, for those two. They had never had a shower before, so that was so fun this morning watching Benjamin go from being afraid to thinking it was fun that the bathroom was raining.

Benjamin likes to copy everything, which is adorable. He is still a little shy and always hides his face when he wants to smile. But he is also very vocal about things. Once we get used to each other and can speak more together, I think he will have us laughing all the time.

> *Anna has a smile worth a million bucks. Her whole face lights up. She is very beautiful. I think it will take some time to earn her trust, but she is willing to listen to us. She is very sweet, and I am looking forward to getting to know who she is.*

> *Everything is so new for them. These kids came from such a different background than James and Kira. They have had very little, and everything is so new. I think they are so brave with all that they have gone through in just the last few days.*

The morning of court arrived quickly. We met at Thomas's office downtown and walked with him to the courtroom in a nearby building. I had already noticed that Benjamin had a lot of energy, and I had, accordingly, filled a backpack with books and paper and crayons and snacks. I also brought the laptop with some movies, in case we were waiting for hours. But as it happened, we did not wait long at all and were soon inside the courtroom.

As I had never really been in court before, this was not at all what I expected. It was more like the judge's office—a small room where the judge sat at her desk, facing rows of chairs. There were three rows facing the desk, and then another row along the side wall. There was a microphone at the corner of her desk. I think my husband sat in the front row with our lawyers, and I sat behind with the two kids.

Aunt Leah and the pastor were sitting somewhere behind me. I spent most of the time trying to keep Benjamin occupied and out of trouble. He tried to pull the curtains out by the window near the judge's desk, and he was climbing on and off chairs. I tried every coloring book I had, and eventually I was able to distract him with some flash cards.

The judge first went over our home study paperwork, asking questions about our work, income, health, etc. She asked me a lot of questions concerning whether or not I was going to be a stay-at-home mom. When she came to the children's paperwork, she became much more concerned. The probation report on the children was half a page in total. She repeatedly asked our lawyer why there was so much information on us and so little on the children.

Here is how I explained court to my family and friends later that day.

10/2/2014

Hello, everyone:

> *Whew! Court is over.*

> *Well, it wasn't what we had hoped for, but we all agree it is going to be a good thing. Let me explain.*

> *The judge decided she did not have enough information on the kids to make a ruling. She said that the information about us is fine. We do not need to be at court again, but she set another court date for November 3, when she wants to see a more complete report from the probation officer (social worker) from Kasese on the children.*

> *This is probably a blessing, because if she feels it is incomplete, then the real problem would be the U.S. Embassy. Another family was just denied Legal Guardianship (permission to leave the country with the kids). If the U.S. Embassy denies it, then the case gets sent to Nairobi for review. That takes one to three months or more, so we want a perfect report that is acceptable, sent to the U.S. Embassy on the first try. I think the judge was very wise in requesting this.*

> *We are actually in a unique position, in that our lawyer already obtained the kids' passports. You have to have the passports in order to complete two major steps: 1) A three-part medical check called International Organization for Migration (IOM), and 2) A U.S. Department of State*

immigration application form, which is online paperwork I must complete here.

So I will be busy getting things done. With any luck and a lot of prayers (hint hint), on November 3, the judge will see complete paperwork and she will QUICKLY give us a ruling. She has been known to take up to seven weeks to give a ruling, but on average, I've heard it's two weeks. Once I have that ruling, and hopefully have completed all the other requirements, I make an appointment at the U.S. Embassy and, hopefully, they will send us right through. With any luck, I will be home mid-November.

We can't afford to go much beyond that, as every government agency here closes mid-December until mid-January, so please, please continue praying for smooth sailing.

Ok, I need to rest my brain. What a day. I hope all are well at home and, hey, I never heard if Notre Dame won its football game last weekend.

Thank you for all your love and support so far. We are so appreciative.

Christine

I don't remember much about the next couple days when my husband was still in Kampala. I came down with some flu virus and was feeling pretty miserable. I was already a little worn out from the kids. They were high energy, fighting a lot and spoke no English. The next morning we took the kids to a Friday market. These are craft markets, mostly for tourists, where men and women sell all kinds of homemade crafts. They are a lot of fun and require bargaining over prices.

Benjamin and Anna each picked out a bright fabric elephant for their bedrooms back home, which my husband packed to take. Each one also picked out one toy to play with at the guest house – a doll and a wire bicyclist.

Tourist Craft Market in Kampala

Saturday came quickly, and we paid Sarah, one of the Ugandan ladies, to watch the kids so we could go to 1000 Cups coffee shop in Kampala to buy some coffee for gifts. I've never been much of a coffee drinker, but Uganda grows such good coffee, and if you go to any café and order a mocha, it comes non-sweetened. They serve it with a bowl of raw sugar, which they also grow in Uganda. It is amazing, and I drank mochas and cappuccinos as much as possible.

1000 Cups of Coffee

Traffic in Kampala

That evening, Charles, our favorite driver, came to take my husband to the airport. I felt pretty low at that point, but knew it was mostly due to my cold.

I already had plans to go to the kids' medical appointments early the next week to get that out of the way. I hoped to get everything done, patiently wait for the judge's ruling in November, and be home for a magical Thanksgiving.

After failing with James and Kira, after going through those weeks of feeling like I did not want to be their mother, feeling it was so wrong, being so disappointed in myself at the time, I knew that this time I had to give myself some time. I knew the kids would not magically bond to me but, more importantly, I now knew I would not magically bond to them.

I hadn't carried them for nine months, I didn't give birth to them and, although I was attached to them, had sympathy for their situation and wanted to love them, I knew it would take my heart time. I now realized that adoption was no Disney movie or "Annie" musical where my heart would instantly love them, nor would they instantly love me as their mother.

I had an image in my head—two images, really. One dream was being in the airport with my two children, holding their hands and being welcomed home by all my family and friends. Second was a vision of our bedtime rituals: giving them baths, putting them in their pj's and reading to them at night in their beds. Those two visions would carry me through the next weeks of tantrums and getting to know each other, loving them where they were, and allowing myself the grace to let my heart slowly attach to them.

I was so blessed by the women staying at the guest house. Their husbands had all gone home as well, and they were in various stages in the process of waiting for that golden visa ticket to go home. Getting past the U.S. Embassy was becoming more and more challenging, and everyone was stressed.

I had been close friends with a woman named Mary, who was adopting two girls. She had a friend from her church who arrived to spend some time helping her with the two girls she was adopting. This woman was a godsend to the house, as she was outside the stress of the process, but had such a heart for the children. She started encouraging all of us by having Bible studies in the evenings. As things got more difficult for everyone, she had us pray and write out scriptures and tape them to the walls of the dining room, where we could be encouraged each day.

The scripture that I was praying was from Romans 5:3-5.

Not only so, but we also glory in our sufferings, because we know that suffering produces perseverance; perseverance, character; and character, hope. And hope does not put us to shame, because God's love has been poured out into our hearts through the Holy Spirit, who has been given to us.

I began having difficulties with Benjamin immediately. He was a very active and a high-energy little boy, which was great. But because he had not had discipline, he was also acting out violently. If he wanted a toy from another child, he would punch and hit until the other child left crying and Benjamin got what he wanted. He was so little, but had so much stubborn, determined energy.

When you are first trying to discipline children you are adopting, it is so incredibly overwhelming. You cannot use any type of corporal punishment at all. As a mother, you are trying desperately to create trust and a loving bond, and to erase any fear of abandonment. Not knowing what their past was like, you never know if they were abused; therefore, you don't know what issues of trust they may have. Then there is the language barrier. Not being able to understand them or explain your actions can be so frustrating. Just navigating getting dressed, meals, playing, bath and bedtime is difficult enough and, without a common language, it was frustrating for me and for them.

The children were also experiencing so many things for the first time: indoor bathrooms, showers, toys, clean clothes, good food every day—all things that can be so much for a child to deal with. On top of that, imagine living in this odd situation of being at a guest house in Africa surrounded by all these white mothers.

Each day became a challenge for me. How do I keep Benjamin occupied so that he is distracted and cannot get into trouble? I was terrified to leave the guest house with the children. When we went to our first International Organization for Migration (IOM) meeting, he was okay in the car but, while waiting in the building, I spent every minute trying to distract him with stickers, books, coloring, toy cars, snacks—anything to keep him from running.

The second appointment was worse. This time he was familiar with the car ride and the building. He kept trying to climb out of the car, trying to open the door and windows even when the car was in motion. I attempted to put him in the middle seat, but he and Anna fought so much. Henry, who was our driver, made sure the windows and doors were locked so Benjamin couldn't get out.

I remember that second appointment. Our first appointment was simply checking in and turning in the paperwork. The second appointment was where the kids were weighed, had their eyesight checked, had blood drawn for an HIV test and got a TB test. The third appointment was to have the TB test read.

I had taken different books and stickers and flash cards and tried to keep Benjamin occupied while we waited for over an hour to be called. There were other kids there waiting as well, all immigrants, from the Sudan or somewhere, on their way to Australia, I'd heard. But Benjamin was quickly losing patience and beginning to fuss. When we were finally called, he had a meltdown and was trying to run away.

I had to carry him to the doctor waiting to meet us. He tried grabbing windows, doorways, chairs – anything on the way he could get a hold of. It's a good thing I didn't have to have *my* blood pressure checked at this point! Anna was brave and did well through the whole checkup, even with having blood drawn and the TB test. When it came for Benjamin's turn, he screamed bloody murder. I couldn't even explain to him why he was having it done.

Finally, we were done, and as we walked back down to the entrance where I had to pick up my passport, Anna whispered something to Benjamin about the armed guards. He took one terrified look and bolted. This was typical of their relationship. They constantly stuck together, but Anna was always whispering to him or telling him something that would set him running. They fought constantly over toys, and their fighting was very physical. I couldn't get through to either one of them, and I dropped into bed every night exhausted.

The other mothers in the house encouraged me and helped with suggestions. Even the African ladies working in the house, who also became such wonderful friends to me, helped as they could. On their advice, I would take Benjamin back to my room when he was throwing one of his many tantrums, and I held him tightly like a baby until he stopped crying, kicking, and hitting. This became an all-day ritual, but I wasn't seeing any results.

In the house, there was kind of an unspoken rule that only the adopting mother would discipline/correct her child, to further the bonding experience. But with Benjamin, for his own safety, other mothers and one father there tried to help. Many had to grab him as he tried to run out the front gate into the road. He tried to climb an iron screen on the dining room door, got to the ceiling and wouldn't come down. I had help getting him down, but and he ran right back and did it again.

I took him back to the room, where he kicked and screamed for an hour and finally calmed down. But as soon as we left the room, he'd walk up to another child and punch him. I spent so much time in my room with him that I felt like I was completely neglecting Anna.

Our room was on the ground floor in the back of the house. Some of the second-floor rooms had a balcony, and I was thankful we did not have one of those rooms. I didn't think I could worry about one more thing! But I caught Benjamin and Anna sneaking up to those rooms and stealing things from other families. I had to forbid them from going upstairs at all. One afternoon, I was sitting at the table while they were coloring, and Benjamin took one look at me, then he bolted. He ran straight upstairs, with me chasing. I got up just in time to see Mark, one of the adopting fathers, grab Benjamin around the waist. Benjamin had one foot over the balcony. I knew then I'd be lucky to keep this boy alive!

I do have one vivid memory of sitting at breakfast across the table from Benjamin when I winked at him, so he kept trying to wink back at me. I kept that sweet image close to my heart, trying to see the promise down the road of having him as my son.

I was worn out. I was so low. I hated myself for being so weak. I was exhausted and unhappy and was not enjoying any part of the day except when I climbed into bed. On October 10, I sent an e-mail to a mother I'd met on my first trip.

> *I am having such a tough time. These kids speak a couple of different languages – not Lugandan and not English. The girl, Anna, bullies her brother, Benjamin, and tells him things to make him mad or scared. He, in turn, throws the most horrific tantrums, throwing himself on the floor, kicking, hitting, screaming, climbing walls, trying to get out of windows or doors of moving vehicles. He runs all the time. The International Organization for Migration this morning was horrible, and when I pick him up, he grabs windows or doors or anything on the walls. I am having a miserable time and wishing I had never made this decision.*

> *I feel like they are both unkind children who for self-preservation only look out for themselves. I know they are kids, I know their life has been unimaginably rough, and I know they are trying to assert some control, which is why they are so bad. But I am feeling like such a failure and that this is all some horrible mistake.*

> *I feel pretty low right now. The last couple of days have been very hard. Benjamin loves being disobedient. He smiles, laughs and does exactly what I tell him not to. The other moms and Grace have been having me carry him to the room when he disobeys and hold him like a baby until he calms down. I'm pretty sure I have a ton of bruises because he kicks, screams, tries to throw himself on the floor, every trick in the book. Then he sobs and cries, but he still doesn't give in. It took two hours yesterday for him to stop fighting me, and two times today took about 30 to 60 minutes each time. Then he just waits to do something bad a little later.*

Anna is older than the other three girls being adopted here. We are not sure by how much. I was told she is 5, but there is no way in the world. She is telling us she is 10, and we are not sure of that either. But she is a bully to her brother and to the other kids. She is sneaky and passive-aggressive. There is so little kindness or real affection in these two. They fight each other nonstop: when they wake up, all day, and when they go to bed. They can barely speak English, but they tattle on each other constantly. Anna has a whine that she uses even with the other girls in telling them what to do.

Today is such a low point for me. I have been on the verge of tears all day. I am such a horrible person. We didn't want James and Kira (and I know logically that they were never ours), but now I am failing again. I am so disgusted with myself and so homesick and miserable all at the same time.

I keep reminding myself that attachment and affection take time. I am not expecting to be attached to them. But they are wearing me down. Even the African women and Henry, a friend, cannot get Benjamin to listen. They tell him he is a bad boy. He doesn't care. He has put himself in so many unsafe positions. He tries to grab electrical wires on the side of the house. I tell him "no" over and over and take him to time out, but he runs right back to grab them. I had an African lady come tell him "no," and he threw himself on the ground and ignored her.

Well, if you have advice, I would love to hear it. You know what it is like to be here without your husband. I hope you don't think I am such an awful person, but I myself am not sure I should even be a mom anymore.

This has been a rough day. I shouldn't send this e-mail,
but I need some advice, so feel free to say anything.

Thanks,
Christine

This is the much-needed response I received from my friend.

Christine,

> *I have been so burdened for you since getting your*
> *e-mail. I am praying hard for you, and I am praying*
> *for how best to encourage you. The first thing that comes*
> *to mind is that you really need help. If you have to stay*
> *through the court process, someone needs to come and*
> *support you.*

> *I would not have been able to survive the last 10 weeks*
> *of my trip without my mom. I still was in the trenches, but*
> *there was a buffer when I hit bottom, and there was an*
> *encourager when I needed one. Whatever it takes to make*
> *that happen, you need to do it! Not only is it hard work,*
> *but it's double hard work because it's two children! If you*
> *don't have to stay, Come Home!*

> *Dealing with the behavioral issues in your own*
> *environment with therapists at your disposal is much easier*
> *than in the charged environment in-country when you*
> *are worried about SO much and without a good support*
> *system. It would not be a failure to come back when it's*
> *time because you are going to need your husband to help*
> *you with that flight for sure!*

> *The other big thing to remember is that none of this*
> *is personal, nor is it a reflection of your parenting ability.*
> *You have been called to parent hurt children, and that is*

hard work. However, you were not called into it alone. The Lord is with you and will equip you for each moment if you put yourself in his hands. The reality of motherhood is that you will constantly fail! Daily, hourly, I fail. I fail in small and in HUGE ways, but grace abounds in my failure! Thankfully, the Lord fills in the gap for me and for my kids. He will do the same for you.

You obviously have a long road ahead of you, but you aren't alone and it's not insurmountable! Give yourself grace, just as the Lord pours out. You don't know Anna and Benjamin yet. You will soon enough know them. You'll know what sets them off, what motivates them, what makes them tick. When that happens, you will feel more maternal. Don't beat yourself up that you aren't feeling overwhelming love. That's normal!

As affection grows in both direction, it gets easier to handle the tantrums. He will allow you to comfort him and you will know how to de-escalate him, too. You just have no history or relationship yet, so it's even more difficult.

Their ages and experiences certainly add to the dynamics, but again...God called you to this. It takes time. My daughter was a disaster the first five weeks! Those first weeks with her were hideous. I was angry, stressed and worried that I'd ruined my and my family's life. I have worried about ruining our family life many times over the last few months. And, quite honestly, I just now (eight months later) feel maternally connected and loving toward her.

I delight in her now, but it's been a VERY LONG road filled with failure after failure. We have done countless things wrong – more wrongs than rights – and yet, attachment has still grown. Just be assured that attachment is not always instant and that's okay! It hasn't even been instant with my bio kids. Motherhood is just weird like that. Pour out the grace God freely gives, girl!

I am praying. Please keep using me as an honest sounding board. Many people will not understand or will downplay the intensity/severity of their and your needs. You need to surround yourselves (even virtually) with people who can take the hard stuff and can support and encourage you as you work through these next hard months of attaching and learning to parent. Find those people and use them. Lean on them and allow them to hold you up when you can't do it for yourself.

Hang in there. Much love!

My friend's e-mail encouraged me with the message that I was not alone. I knew the other mothers at the guest house had been with their children longer and had gone through their tantrums and struggles already. But it was so difficult to be going through this a second time, alone, and feeling like such a failure.

The climax came on Saturday, October 11. The other families in the house had decided to go to church together on Sunday morning, then out to dinner. The Ugandan ladies who worked at the guest house had Sunday evening off, which they greatly deserved, so there were no meals served in the evening. Often we just ordered pizza delivered to the house. You may be surprised that you could get pizza delivered in Africa! It was very similar to American pizza, and I highly recommend the ham and pineapple.

Anyhow, I argued that there was no way I could take the kids to church and a restaurant, as I couldn't control them in the guest house. But the other mothers all assured me that they would help, and it would be fine. The day went on as normal, as I constantly watched and disciplined Benjamin for hitting and Anna for instigating. After dinner, the kids were all playing outside. The mothers would often pull up plastic chairs in the evening and talk before we gathered all the kids to our rooms for bath and bed.

But as I walked out of the dining hall into the courtyard, I could not find Anna or Benjamin anywhere. They were not playing with the other kids, not in our room, nor upstairs. I looked in the bathrooms and through the whole house and was worried they had run out the gate. The other mothers began looking as well. One of the adults found them in the garden that was adjacent to the courtyard, divided by a brick wall and accessed by a small door at the end of the property.

The kids were not allowed back there. It was used by the guard and his wife to grow some small things, and to cut down some jackfruit and bananas. They also also went there to butcher chickens. It was a large space full of plants and scrubs. There could be broken glass, trash and even snakes; therefore, no kids were allowed. Anna and Benjamin knew this, as they had tried before.

This time, I think they knew they had crossed the line by making us all worry and hunt for them. When one of the women found them, the kids immediately ran to the shed at the back of the property. This was a small building where the guard kept tools, but also had a "squat" attached, which is the traditional bathroom that he and his wife used. Anna ran in, slammed the door shut and locked it from the inside. As she slammed the door, it caught Benjamin's fingers, and he immediately began screaming. He was fine, but I think knowing they were in trouble, and with Anna hiding, it was overwhelming.

Mary stood by the shed door, told me she would wait for Anna, and I should go get Benjamin ready for bed. I was near tears because the humiliation of not being able to control my own kids (even though they had been mine for only two weeks) was breaking me. I silently picked up Benjamin and took him to the room, started the shower going and began to undress him. I had him undressed except for his underwear when he bolted out the door. He then began running through the house mostly naked, from room to room, darting away from adults – both white families and Ugandan staff who were all trying to catch him.

I remember sitting outside in the courtyard on the step, my head in my hands, exhausted, overwhelmed and at a loss. Eventually, Anna cracked the door open, and Mary grabbed her. Someone else finally caught the little naked troublemaker, and I headed back to my room. On the way, one of the mothers said, "Sorry, Christine, but I don't think you should take them to church tomorrow. I don't think even all of us can keep them out of trouble."

I felt crushed, and all the energy and optimism left me that night. The next morning, I tried to face another day, hoping for the best. My new friends, Mark and Renee, stayed back at the house with me. They were in their early 50s and had a set of triplets at home in high school. They decided to adopt Ian, a little guy about three years old, who was born with physical disabilities but gifted with the ability to steal your heart!

I was thankful for their company. Renee was a blessing, and knowing that I was at my breaking point, she was kind enough to color and do flash cards with the kids, keeping them busy. I think she was trying to play cards with them as well. That was pretty funny, and since Benjamin didn't know his numbers, (or speak English) he just assumed he won every hand.

I was sitting nearby checking my e-mail. (In Uganda, internet is wireless, not through phone lines. Instead, you buy airtime on a flash drive and plug it into your computer. You just add minutes to the flash as you run out.) I received an e-mail from my husband, stating that Pastor Mark was calling him at 3 a.m., asking for money, asking for him to get donations to send. This was incredibly unsettling, as we didn't even have guardianship of the kids yet, and to have him asking for money could give the appearance we were buying children.

I had already explained to the pastor and my lawyers that we could not in any way be giving money for these children. We could give a donation after the adoption was finalized in the United States, but not beforehand. I was irritated and really began to distrust this pastor's intentions. There seemed to be something underhanded and out of place with what he was doing. Grace, the Ugandan lady who runs the guest house, was often someone I went to for advice, so I told her about the phone calls. She was also immediately suspicious. She had never heard of another family having this issue. She decided to question Anna in her language one more time.

This time the results were shocking. Anna said that "Aunt Leah" is her mother! At first, even Grace thinks the child is misunderstanding, since in Ugandan culture they often call other relatives who care for them "mother." But Anna assured Grace that Leah is her mother. She says she is the one who breastfed her, and she even made motions imitating breastfeeding, so there is no doubt.

Then she went on to say that she has four brothers. She has two older brothers named Chance and Baraka, and her two younger brothers are Benjamin and Mika. I'd met Mika and one of the older boys, whom I was told were Leah's only children.

Grace had me call an American couple who were adopting a little girl from Uganda and who had been living in Uganda as missionaries for over a year with two of their other children. After getting their advice, I called a Ugandan man named David. He was an investigator. After talking briefly on the phone, he came to the guest house within a couple of hours.

David was thin, medium height, probably in his mid-thirties. I found out that he ran his own school, for which he was constantly trying to raise funds. He had twins at home. He really seemed to love kids.

I gave David a Coke, we sat on the porch, and I told him what had happened up to that point. I explained how I met my lawyer, my initial meeting with the pastor and his abrasive behavior, the judge's decision in court that we didn't have enough of a report on the kids, and Anna's startling statement that Leah was her mother.

Benjamin came at this point and climbed in David's lap. David asked him a question in his language, and Benjamin answered and pointed across the porch table at me. David said he had asked Benjamin where he had lived, and with whom he lived before coming here. Benjamin answered that he lived in the village with his mother until this muzungu, or white woman, had come and taken him away and brought him here.

All the pieces instantly fell into place concerning Benjamin's behavior. I had stolen him from his mother. At first, the kids were in a

new place with new things to enjoy and distract them, but as the weeks went on, they realized that I was not taking them back to their mom. It was no wonder that he was constantly trying to escape and misbehaving. He must have had so much anger and fear and frustration.

Even now, I cannot imagine what it must have felt like to be four years old, separated from his mother and brothers, away from his home with a house full of strange white people who did not speak your language. On top of this, the food at the guest house was so different from what he was used to, to say nothing of taking him to court, then to doctors to get shots. The poor kids must have been scared, confused, homesick. It's no surprise that they were acting out and getting into so much trouble.

When Jack and Connie returned from church, I told them all that I had learned, and how I had met with David. They agreed this was the right course of action, but they also wanted to contact their friend Abdul. Abdul runs Jack's farm, his property outside of Kampala, halfway to Entebbe.

Abdul is an intimidating figure – over six feet tall and powerfully built with a deep voice. But soon I found he is quick to break into a smile and laughter. He is the same age I am, is married and blessed with four children. He never finished high school and yet is truly one of the wisest men I have ever met. In addition to his intelligence, he has an intuition regarding people, which makes him invaluable to many. He is often asked to help the police diffuse tense situations, although he does not work on the police force. There is no one like Abdul, and I am so incredibly blessed that now I can call him my friend.

Abdul came, and we sat in Jack and Connie's living room. I described the situation, and I remember being nervous, kind of in shock as to what was happening. Yet I was not even fully aware of the precarious position I was in. Abdul immediately assessed the situation and realized that I needed to be protected in a way that I could not be accused of being involved with stealing children. He made arrangements to contact me later that week.

In the meantime, he advised me to go nowhere with the children, and not to let them outside the guest house grounds at all. He also

advised me not to contact or speak with my lawyers, not to let them know what we had learned yet. On Wednesday, he called and made arrangements to pick me up with his friend Isma who is the Assistant Superintendent of Police (ASP).

Isma is medium height and build, somewhat soft-spoken and thoughtful. He is college educated and has a degree as a social worker, but he decided he wanted to serve as a police officer. Wednesday afternoon I met with him and Abdul once again in Jack and Connie's living room, repeating my story to Isma this time. Isma and Abdul decided they needed to take me and the children immediately to the closest police station to file a report. That way, even while I was waiting on David to return with the investigation, I would have an official record of what happened and how I discovered the truth. This would protect me from being charged with child trafficking until I was able to return the children to their mother.

I had no clue what to expect. Abdul and Isma decided it was best to go to the police station in Kabalagala. This was only a few minutes' drive away, maybe twenty minutes' walk from the guest house. The police station is across the street from the Johnrich grocery store. The station is surrounded with barbed wire fence and the entrance has an officer manning a strip with spikes across the ground that they slide out of the way to let cars enter.

The police station is a small building with three rooms and is surrounded by small barracks where officers live. On the side of the building, a camouflage tent was set up. An officer in a blue camouflage uniform was coming out of the tent, adjusting his uniform. There were many other police officers standing outside as well. I'm sure I made quite the spectacle, a white woman with two Ugandan children, escorted by two men. At first I couldn't even get Benjamin out of the car because of the two giant turkeys that were wandering by the car and the numerous dogs lounging outside the station.

We were led inside to a back room that was lit by light coming through two windows. There were some plastic chairs and a long table covered in stacks of paperwork and case files. Abdul and Isma initiated the meeting by explaining why I was there and what had happened and

why I needed to make a statement. The police asked me a few questions. I spent most of the time trying to pay attention, not pass out, and keep Benjamin in his seat. Benjamin by now was quickly bored with the same flash cards, coloring books and toy cars.

For awhile, we sat in the room alone as Abdul and Isma went into another room to speak with the Kabalagala police. Eventually, a woman officer came back to take my statement. The process in total took three hours. After an hour, Benjamin would no longer listen to me at all and was wandering the police station at will. When a statement is taken, police use blank paper and a ruler to make margins. They write out everything and have me sign and date each page. My statement was eight pages. Toward the end, we were all exhausted. By this time, Benjamin was sitting in my lap, and Anna was next to me. Somehow Benjamin had found a police ink pad and had thumbprinted himself and had his prints everywhere in the building. Oh, my goodness! I was exhausted.

The rest of the week went by in a daze. By this time, I was fairly confident these were not my children, and it took some of the pressure off feeling like I was failing. The other mothers and fathers who were in the guest house were such a blessing to me. They decided that since Benjamin was such a handful, we should all be responsible for him. What an amazing group! There is something so special about those families who had such strength and compassion. I admire them so much.

On Saturday, the investigator, David, gave me his report. He went to the villages where the kids were supposed to be from and found no relatives to these children at all, and no grave sites. He went to Kasese and carefully did an investigation there. The pastor was out of town, and he made sure not to speak to the aunt because he did not want to "tip her off" that he was investigating. Instead, he spoke with her neighbors and quickly got to the truth.

Leah was the children's mother, not their aunt. She had six children and was very poor, often relying on the pastor and the church for food and basic necessities. I believe she sold fish as a living and did not earn much at all. The pastor saw an opportunity to profit, so he lied to Leah, saying that an American family wanted to sponsor Benjamin and Anna in Kampala for boarding school, and they would come back and stay with her between terms. Leah was beginning to suspect he was lying and that we were not sponsoring, but taking, her children. But the pastor had warned all the villagers around her not to speak to her, not to give away the truth. So they isolated her.

After showing David's investigation results to Isma and Abdul, we formulated a plan. Jacob, my lawyer's assistant, had been calling me on Friday, asking me to meet him and give him more funds for the new probation report. Abdul now told me to set up a time to meet Thomas and Jacob at their office on Monday morning to turn over those funds. In the meantime, Abdul, Isma, and a handful of armed policemen and women would leave Sunday at 3 a.m. and drive straight to Kasese. They would find the mother and convince her to come back with them, and then on Monday we would all confront my lawyers together.

I had arranged for Leah to stay at a guest house nearby on Sunday evening. All day I waited with the other families for them to return. At one point, Abdul called and said they would be coming to the house in the evening so Leah could see her children before going to the guest house. I remember sitting on a plastic chair in the evening with the other families – waiting. We were watching the kids, talking about how crazy this was all becoming. Then I received a phone call from Jacob, and he sounded very strange over the phone. He asked if everything was okay, because he had just heard (from whom I don't know) that four-year-old Benjamin was in jail.

What?! Seriously, they couldn't come up with a better story? I assured him the kids were fine. He didn't believe me, so I put Anna on the phone. I knew he was fishing for information. We found out later that Jacob had been trying to call Leah all day as well, but Abdul advised her not to answer. Someone in the village must have tipped them off that Leah left with police.

That evening, all the moms decided to meet in the living room of the guest house for prayer. But the truth is, all we did was talk and laugh until we were all crying. I think God knew we needed some relief and a little joy. All of these families were going through stress with their adoptions, and here they were, helping me cope with mine. I will always cherish that night and those friendships. At about 9 p.m., the guard got a call from Abdul to open the gate. After the van pulled in, I felt like we were in a movie. The driver, Abdul, Leah, her son Mika, and about four heavily armed police in white uniforms piled out. The police were all carrying AK-47s.

I nervously escorted them to the back of the house where my room was, and everyone piled in this tiny room. The kids were sleeping next to each other on the bottom bunk. It took a little bit to wake them up; they were so confused about what was going on. After a bit, Anna seemed to understand and got out of bed. I left them for awhile to get reacquainted. After speaking with Abdul and with Jack and Connie, we decided it was best that Leah stay the night with the kids here at the guest house. I just gathered a few things and slept in an empty room upstairs. Before going to bed, we got Leah and Mika some basic toiletries and some food. I still hadn't seen her smile or relax, but I could not even imagine all she was going through.

The next morning, Grace spent an hour with Leah, talking to her in their language and explaining all that was happening. What Grace relayed to me was shocking. That first day I had met the kids in Kasese, Leah had asked Jacob and the pastor where we were taking the kids, and they had said Kampala. She didn't believe them. She said she "had bitterness in her stomach" and that she had been fasting for three weeks, crying out to God, asking where her kids were.

The pastor and Jacob had told her the day I left with the kids that she would see them at court, and they would explain more about the arrangements then. But by then, she didn't know whom to trust, and she even thought I was part of it. They used fear and intimidation and her poverty to trick her and take advantage of her. When I think of her crying out to God, asking where her children were, I am still stunned.

When we explained the plan about confronting my lawyers, which I think also scared her, she didn't say much, and her anxiety paralyzed her. Before leaving the guest house, Jack and Connie, Grace, all the parents in the house, Abdul, Isma and Leah all gathered in a circle on the drive and held hands. Jack started praying over all of us and what we were about to do. It was not the last time that I would feel so grateful for staying at this guest house and for the faith and wisdom of Jack and Connie!

When we arrived at my lawyers' office, Isma and Abdul told me to go in with Leah, and they would wait until my lawyers arrived. Then I was to text them, and they would walk in. Thomas's conference room was a narrow rectangular room with a bank of windows on one side. The conference table took up most of the space and left little area to maneuver around. Leah and the kids all sat beneath the windows and I sat on the other side. We were on the second floor, and the noise below on the streets could be heard.

When my lawyers walked in, the shock on their faces was unmistakable. I texted Abdul right away, but it took them a few minutes to arrive, so it was up to me to be the first to speak. Thomas asked why the aunt was there. He did not speak the language Leah spoke, so he was asking me. All I remember saying was, "You mean their mother?!"

When they heard that, Thomas and Jacob feigned being shocked and said they had no idea. Then they began to blame her, saying she was a liar and was selling her children. I immediately told them I knew that was not true, that she was angry and had also been lied to.

At this point, Abdul and Isma arrived. Upon learning that Isma was a policeman, Thomas and Jacob's behavior changed to great concern. Abdul sat at one end of the table to my right, the lawyers to my left. Isma sat across from me, next to Leah and the kids. Abdul assessed the situation very quickly, and he told Thomas and Jacob he wanted Leah to explain what had happened in her language. He said he wanted Jacob to translate for us what she was saying, but he warned Jacob that he (Abdul) also knew her language and exactly what she was saying.

So Jacob had to translate the story and how he had lied to her and told her that these whites were taking her kids to sponsor in a boarding school in Kampala. Jacob had to admit his guilt; he was caught in his lies. Thomas was visibly distressed, as he claimed he knew none of this, that he would never deal with trafficking kids because he owned his own law practice and could lose his business. He was very apologetic after that.

We sat there negotiating over an hour, and Leah was so distressed she sat with a shawl over her head most of the time. The kids were quickly bored and began fighting. I pulled out two suckers and gave one to Benjamin and one to Anna. They informed me that two-year-old Mika needed one as well. As soon as I handed him one, he chucked it out of the window onto the street below. The kids kept fighting, so I had Anna come sit next to me.

I was nervous and stressed and trying so hard to follow the discussion. I had Anna next to me, her sandal in her hand whacking Benjamin in the head as he sat under the table with his leg in the air kicking Anna. Leah still had her shawl over her head. At this point, Abdul asked Leah to take the kids in the waiting room while we finished talking.

After a bit, Abdul asked me to wait in the waiting room as well. I found Leah with her shawl over her head, Mika with most of his clothes off, a waiting room full of people and Benjamin and Anna nowhere to be found. I went in the hallway where Anna was walking, telling me Benjamin had run down the stairs. The stairs led to the open door, straight outside to a busy street in downtown Kampala. I'm still surprised I didn't have a stroke.

I quickly ran down the stairs when I saw the little guy stomping his way back up them. As soon as he saw me, he turned around and tried to run straight down again. Another Ugandan lady coming up the stairs grabbed him and brought him to me, talking about a naughty child. Oh, my goodness, I carried him back to the waiting room.

When we returned, I stood in the hallway with Anna. She was bent slightly over with Mika on her back. This little girl, this ten-year-old child. I was seeing a different side to her now. Since her mother had shown up the night before, she had been busy getting her mother food, helping her with Mika, acting so responsible and hardworking. Even in the midst of my stress, I realized that she had a hard life. I now knew she was ten, a middle child, the only daughter among five brothers. She would most likely spend her life helping her mother care for them: cooking, cleaning and working. She would not have much of a childhood. Yet she was smiling that same smile, with those mischievous eyes, always so ready to laugh.

Soon I was called back into the conference room where Abdul relayed to me that in order to save his business, Thomas was in complete agreement to do another, ethical adoption. This time he would do the work, and not Jacob. He also agreed to pay for my stay at the guest house and all travel expenses I would have related to the adoption. He would expedite the process and try to have me home by Christmas. Furthermore, any correspondence between me and my lawyer would also include Isma, and Abdul would come to any meetings I would have with my lawyer.

I was tired, and in my mind I had already been thinking ahead to buying tickets and heading home. But I also knew that my husband and I were broke. We couldn't afford to start this process again. Part of me also dreaded the thought of going home again—a failure, empty-handed, no children. God had guided me through this process so far and no harm had come to me, and two families had been reunited.

With this new guarantee of Thomas covering expenses and promising an ethical adoption, it seemed too good a blessing to pass up. At least this was what I decided over the next few days. I prayed about it and felt I could confidently stay longer and see what would happen. At the very least, I had a return plane ticket for mid-November, and I could wait until then to see what was in store.

We arrived back at the guest house and began to pack up a suitcase for the kids to take with them. I put all the clothes I'd bought them, plus toys, books, and toiletries. I collected some of my clothes for Leah. Connie let me go through a bin of clothes that families had left, and the other mothers in the house went through their clothes for both Leah and Mika. I also gave Leah 100,000 shillings, which is less than $50, to help her get started on her own business selling used clothing.

Before leaving the lawyers' office, we had made it clear that they would pay for a private car to take Leah and the kids back to Kasese, since she was still too stressed to ride on a longer journey in a hot and dusty taxi. Jacob actually arrived driving a car; whether it was his or Thomas's, I was unsure.

Before they left, I took a few pictures of Leah and the kids. Leah was still looking distraught. I'm sure she was exhausted and probably still not trusting anyone at this point. I couldn't blame her. Little Mika clung to her legs, probably with no idea what was going on. Benjamin and Anna were all smiles and so excited. They had a suitcase full of clothes, books and toys. They were getting to ride in a car and, best of all, they had the security and joy of being back with their mother and were on their way home.

They lived in such poverty, and Leah was a target for abuse and being taken advantage of. She had to support six children on her own. But she was their mother, and her love for them was great – so great that she fasted for three weeks, crying out to God to find two of her children. She may have been overwhelmed and distraught, but she had great faith and courage, and her children were reunited with her, in part, because of it.

As they drove away, I felt relief, like a huge weight had been lifted. I was no longer in fear of arrest or being accused of trafficking children. I was no longer in fear of losing Benjamin or fearing for his safety.

But there were also feelings of loss and sadness at the thought of another failure. I had so many doubts that began to arise about my fitness as a mother. But mostly, I felt relief, and I slept better than I had in days.

Chapter 4: Cautiously Optimistic: Paul and Sasha

Trust in the Lord with all your heart and lean not on your own understanding; in all your ways submit to him, and he will make your paths straight.
Proverbs 3:5-6

In the next few days, I had two leads on how to begin searching for orphans. I was determined now that I would meet the children before accepting a referral, and I would hire an investigator to thoroughly check their backgrounds before I signed any papers. A friend from home had contact information for a man at a "babies' home," which is different from an orphanage in that it is primarily for babies and toddlers.

Mary, who was adopting two girls at the guest house, had become a very good friend of mine. She introduced me to Roger, who was the social worker she worked with. Roger came to the guest house and said he knew of some reputable programs for adoptable orphans. I sent both of these leads with the contact information to Thomas, my attorney.

He immediately said for me to go ahead and follow up on them and keep him informed. I was surprised, since I had had no part in previous searches but, as I trusted him so little, I thought perhaps this was the best course of action anyhow. At one point in the next few weeks, I met with Thomas in his office, accompanied by Abdul. I showed Thomas that I had brought a receipt book with me. I asked if I should just get receipts when possible, or make them out and get signatures and have him reimburse me if I was going to do the work for the referrals. He said yes, that was fine.

I started working with Roger since I didn't know much about the other babies' home or the contact I was given from there. I gave him directions about wanting one or two children, age five or under with good health – and they must be "total orphans." Roger said he had a contact, a probation officer, who had informed him of a foster care program in a village called Kassanda, near the larger city of Mubende. He said the probation officer had told him that there were many legitimate and total orphans who were in the program.

The program gave a small stipend to an adult to foster the orphans. Roger had been assured they were adoptable and, as I knew that the U.S. Embassy and our last judge were placing great emphasis on a complete and accurate report by a probation officer, it seemed to be a good lead. I asked Roger to go ahead and get more information on available orphans in this program.

In the meantime, I was getting to know the families in the house better, as well as some of my Ugandan friends. I especially became close with Mary and the two girls she was adopting, ages four and six. Roger was often their driver, as well as social worker, so we hired him one day to drive us to the Ziwa Rhino Sanctuary, which was a few hours' drive from Kampala. Rhinos were wiped out in Uganda by 1982 by poachers. Ziwa Rhino Sanctuary is a privately owned 7,000 hectares (17,298 acres) of savannah begun in 2005. They began with six rhinos and, with their successful breeding program, now have 15. The rhinos live undisturbed in the sanctuary, but are guarded from poachers by armed gamekeepers.

We arrived midday and trekked with a guide through the grassland to a cluster of trees where we quietly came upon three juvenile rhinos. According to the guide, rhinos are solitary as adults, but juveniles still stick together. Since the day was hot, they were napping in the shade. Rhinos do not see well, and they can scare easily, so we approached very quietly through the trees. At one point, one of the very relaxed rhinos passed some gas, and the girls bolted in fear. Roger and the guide had to catch them and assure them – silently – that we were fine. Needless to say, I found this hysterical.

One rhino did catch wind of us and nervously stood up. We froze among the trees until she relaxed and laid back down. I was in heaven! It was like coming upon sleeping dinosaurs. Their thick grey hide is crisscrossed with scars and marks. The many wrinkles around their eyes and mouth give them character and personality. The ears, which seemed so small atop their massive heads, were twitching to keep flies away and to listen closely for unusual sounds. The sunlight coming through the trees and the sounds of insects and trill of birds lent this mini-safari all the charm and magic desired. I've been a zookeeper, but seeing these great creatures in Africa in their native habitat was amazing. The day was a welcome relief from the stress of the past weeks.

Ziwa Rhino Sanctuary

Ziwa Rhino Sanctuary

After the rhino trek, we drove in the sanctuary to an outdoor restaurant. We passed small rental cabins and parked at a beautiful outdoor, completely open-air restaurant. There was a bar along one side and we sat at a long wooden table. The roof was held up by tall wooden posts and tree trunks. The center of the restaurant floor was terraced with stone steps and had wooden chairs and coffee tables made from the cross-section of tree trunks.

The atmosphere was relaxed and beautiful – perfect for a safari. To the side was a pool, a small playground and two Western-style bathrooms which, although clean, were inhabited by many lizards! At the back of the restaurant was the "kitchen" of sorts. It was completely open, consisting of a countertop, a shelf with some ingredients and two portable stovetops. Behind the restaurant were a few primitive homes surrounded by small trees, and chickens wandering at will.

The man at the bar left to get the cook, who probably lived in one of the nearby houses. There was no menu, and the cook simply asked if we liked pork. He was a middle-aged Ugandan man wearing a striped polo shirt and khaki pants. He cooked like a chef in a very expensive restaurant. I can still say that it was one of the best meals I have had. With limited tools, he cooked us each a pork chop with gravy, carrots and other root vegetables, and steamed rice. For dessert, we each received a plate beautifully arranged with fresh pineapple, watermelon and mango, topped with chocolate mousse and peanuts. The chef's skill was another reminder to me of the talent and skill found everywhere in Uganda, even in this remote place in a rhino sanctuary.

What a joy to meet these beautiful Ugandan people!

On the ride home, I sat in the back of the car with Mary's daughters, who were tired from a long day. Soon their silliness turned to sleepiness as they both fell asleep with their heads in my lap. These girls, along with their mother, Mary, will always have a special place in my heart. Her older daughter, who had to grow up at the young age of six, was such a strong-hearted, beautiful girl. I learned the meaning of courage from this child, who has such a strong faith and desire to do good.

Mary's younger daughter has taught me that even with a hard life, there is always a reason to find joy. She loved to be silly and could laugh about anything. She decided that day to call me "Uncle Grace," which immediately sent both girls into giddy laughter. I have no idea why it was so funny, but it stills makes me smile thinking about it. Spending time with these girls helped my heart to slowly heal and gave me hope that my children were out there, waiting for me.

Soon after that week, Roger called saying that he had some files on children for me to look at. He came to the guest house, and we sat at the dining table to look over three possible referrals. The first was a girl named Allen, who was a little older and outside of my approved age group. The next was a boy of four or five years old, and a little girl of two. Paul, the boy, was an orphan being cared for by his aunt, Kate. His parents had died of HIV. He initially had gone to live in a faraway village with an aunt and uncle, but Kate was able to visit him after about a year had passed and found that he had been neglected and abused and made to do hard labor. She was very poor herself but couldn't leave him, so she brought him back to Kassanda and asked a village pastor, Pastor Luke, for help.

She was able to enroll in a foster care program and was given a house and a little money to help care for Paul. She had a job cleaning a church and, one evening after service, she found an abandoned child outside.

This was Sasha, who was little more than one year old at the time. Kate and the pastor took Sasha to the local counsel to try to locate her family. Having no luck, they then took her to the police, who filed a report and sent Sasha back with Kate.

Sasha also became enrolled in a foster program owned by Pastor Luke and Ruth, a social worker. Roger had met them both while investigating the possible referrals. After looking over the paperwork, I decided to meet the children. Paul was a complete orphan with no living parents. I hesitated to take him away from an aunt, but if she really couldn't care for him and wanted him adopted, I could at least meet him. Sasha had been abandoned.

I knew from other families that if I accepted this referral, I would be required to pay for radio and newspaper advertisements to look for Sasha's family. Knowing that an effort had already been made and a police report filed was good news. I was told that Kate gave Sasha her name, as nothing was known about her when she was found. Neither child spoke English, but I knew we could navigate around that.

I agreed to go on a Thursday to Kassanda with Roger's friend. Mary also agreed to go for moral support, and she hired a babysitter for the girls. Wednesday we hired my friend Charles to drive us around Kabalagala (near the guest house) in order to buy school supplies to take to the foster home.

Until it came time to leave on Thursday, I was a nervous wreck. After failing to adopt the last four children, I couldn't imagine choosing my own children now. I was nervous about making the wrong decision and choosing the wrong ones. Wednesday night, I was in the guest house, hanging out with two other adopting mothers. Jack was on the computer working on a sermon, as he was preaching at one of the churches on Sunday. Somehow, Jack sensed my nervousness. I hadn't even spoken to him about it. He called me over and said he wanted to tell me what his dad always told him when he was young. "You can't steer a parked car." He went on to explain, "You have to move in the direction you think God wants you to move in and listen for the Holy Spirit." He told me to memorize the verses of Proverbs 3:5-6.

> *Trust in the Lord with all your heart,*
> *and lean not on your own understanding;*
> *in all your ways submit to him,*
> *and he will make your paths straight.*

Jack's advice calmed my nerves and really gave me the courage and confidence to move forward, knowing that I wasn't going to make a mistake if I was listening to the Holy Spirit. Memorizing that Scripture became a shield, a protection. I awoke the next morning nervous, but excited and hopeful. Roger and his friend Nicholas picked us up the next morning. Mary and I piled in the back of the car. I was not feeling my best physically, as I had a bacterial infection (which was to come back and plague me a number of times while I was in Uganda). My stomach was upset, and my chest ached, making it hard to breathe. Both Mary and Connie had gone through the same symptoms recently, so I knew what it was. I took Imodium and water and didn't eat much all day in order to make it without being too sick.

It was a hot and dusty drive. Doubtless, we made an interesting spectacle in traffic: two Ugandan men driving two white ladies in the back seat. At one point, some boda (motorcycle) drivers said something through the window to Roger and Nicholas about the muzungus, and they all laughed. I can only imagine what they said, which required eye rolling from us. Some things don't really need to be translated.

The drive was a few hours traveling through the larger city of Mubendi, then to the small village of Kassanda. We went to the foster home office first to meet Ruth, the social worker, and Pastor Luke. The office was basically a freestanding open stall with a dirt floor, a single desk and a few chairs. The walls were covered in pieces of large white paper that had the foster program's mission written all over in marker ink. Some posters described the group's definition of vulnerable children. Other posters described their goal and how they determine to help children. It was done in a primitive way, but I was impressed. This felt more genuine than my last experience.

After the introductions with Pastor Luke and Ruth, we left the school supplies we had bought for the program and piled into the car to drive the short distance to meet Paul and Sasha. The house they lived in, cared for by Kate, was only minutes away. It was halfway down a large hill, below a boarding school. Kate's house was next to another house in a small clearing. There were small trees and bushes, a little garden, and chickens were running around. It was really beautiful. Everything was clean and neat, although there really wasn't much to speak of.

Kate's house was a small brick rectangular building with two doorways. Inside were some blankets on the floor, a small table, a few clothes and a yellow plastic water container. Kate appeared to be in her late thirties or early forties. She was a beautiful woman, who seemed very confident and was pleasant to me – smiling, holding my hands and giving me a hug. The difference was so striking from meeting the mother of Benjamin and Anna. Paul and Sasha were both wearing worn and ragged clothing. Sasha was very dirty. Neither child had shoes on.

Here is the e-mail I sent to family and friends describing the day.

Good morning,

    About the kids:

    About two years ago, Paul's parents died. He has one older brother, who I think is named Roger. At the funeral of their parents, a family took the boys home. A year later, their aunt was able to travel and visit them. She told us when she found them she was very upset. They were covered in jiggers, they were not being cared for, and they were being used for hard labor, doing the work of adults. From the way she spoke (this was all translated), we could see she was very irritated. I think the boys were treated very badly. So although she was poor, she took Paul, and her sister, in another village took his brother.

    She went to a foster program in Kassanda and requested help. This is a newer program that gives some support for someone like this aunt to care for kids. We met Pastor Luke and Ruth, two people who work with the program. They gave the aunt a little two-room house and helped her with some food and school fees. She is caring for six children.

About six months ago or more, after an evening church service ended, the people came out of church to find an abandoned baby girl. She was taken to police and a report was filed, but parents were not found. So she was given to a foster program in Kassanda and they placed her with Paul's aunt. She named her Sasha. She has been with the aunt for six months now. We are all guessing she is between eighteen months and two years.

The glaring difference from yesterday's meeting and the last two situations is the following:

1) When I first met Pastor Mark and Ruth in the "office," I was impressed by the walls. They were covered in poster board signs that had all of their goals and values written up. What vulnerable children are, how to care for them, what they deserve, how to protect them, what basic needs they have, what spiritual needs they have, etc.

2) When we drove to meet the aunt and Paul and Sasha, the pastor came, but he didn't say anything. Remember our last encounter with a man calling himself a pastor. Before that man would even show us the kids, he was demanding money from us.

3) The aunt came up to us, smiling and thanking us and welcoming us, holding my hand and being so friendly and sweet. Remember our last two situations with mothers who either felt they had to give up their children, or a mother (who we thought was an aunt) who was angry because she was being forced by lies into selling her children.

4) Roger translated, but he also asked the aunt if she understood that adoption was permanent, that we would be taking the kids to America. He also asked if she understood that we would not be giving her any money. We weren't buying the children and the adoption was only for the sake of the children. She understood, and she said she understood she would be giving up guardian rights.

We spent more than an hour sitting with the kids, giving them treats and bottles of water. When we finally had to leave, we went to a market where we (Mary and I) bought rice, bread, sugar, flour, cooking oil, tea, soap, washing soap, toothpaste, toothbrushes, butter, jam, lotion, biscuits (cookies), a soccer ball and toy car. Ruth took everything to the aunt later. Then we drove another hour to meet the probation officer. So already, the concerns I had from the last two cases were being taken care of.

Love you all,
Christine

Meeting Paul and Sasha was difficult, since I felt such pressure to make a decision, to hear what God wanted me to do. They were children: vulnerable and adorable. They didn't speak any English. As Sasha warmed up (giving her candy helped), she began bossing other nearby children around, which was hilarious. She was a sassy two year old for sure! Paul was quiet and shy, sitting apart, but watching me.

There was a moment when I was taking pictures and he gave me a smile. It melted my heart. That smile was it; it made me feel so protective and wanting to care for these two. It was that smile that felt like a confirmation that these children were supposed to be my children. I was tired, not feeling well, emotionally bruised and scared, but in that smile I felt a trust. I felt that this was right.

Because the U.S. Embassy and the judges were now demanding more in-depth reports from probation officers, and signatures from the probation officer in charge of the district, Roger felt we should introduce ourselves to the Mubendi probation officer. Kassanda was in the Mubendi district, and we had to go through Mubendi to return home anyway. The head probation officer was a woman by the name of Miriam, which felt like another confirmation, as that is my sister's name and the middle name I had planned to give to Anna.

Roger received word that the probation officer was in a small village outside Mubendi, and we headed there immediately. It was such a fun drive. The landscape in this part of Uganda is beautiful. We were off the main highway, driving on a dirt road up and down steep hills. I remember small trees giving shade to men who were tending cattle or goats. At one point, we had to stop the car, as a large herd of cattle was coming down the road at us. I could have reached out and grabbed their long horns.

As we neared the village where the probation officer was reported to be, we passed by very traditional Ugandan homes with animals untethered and walking around. There were men and women outside working or relaxing, while small children ran around. Soon we were near the main road – the heart of the village with a few shops. But as we turned a corner, we had to come to a complete halt. There had to be a few hundred people gathered for a soccer game.

We found out later that because of heavy rains, their Independence Day celebration had been postponed to this day. To celebrate, the whole village and surrounding ones had gathered, along with many huge trucks with men in camouflage uniforms. Were they local military troops? We couldn't drive any farther because there were so many people. It appeared that most of them had never seen white women before because they all stared at us in disbelief and curiosity. Many came close to the car to get a better look.

One such man was next to the driver's door, and he was visibly intoxicated. Roger decided his best move was to reverse the car to get out of the congestion. As soon as he started to roll backwards, the drunk man began screaming because we had slowly rolled onto his foot! The entire crowd was now staring and laughing. Roger completely panicked and pulled forward. The drunk man was so relieved, he began laughing with the crowd and hobbled off. I imagine he felt it the next day!

After calling her cell phone, we were able to find Miriam, the probation officer, in the crowd. But because of the crowd, I didn't even get out of the car. We shook hands through the window and that was about it. We headed back to Kampala, getting there after dark. It was a long, exhausting day, but I felt confident that I had found my children at last.

The next few weeks, Roger was collecting paperwork, probation reports and other documents. He and I met with Thomas, my lawyer, at which time I brought a list of expenses and receipts for him to reimburse. Thomas promptly refused to pay for any of it, accusing me of outrageous expenses and even of trafficking children myself. Abdul met my lawyer to try and figure out what was going on. Abdul determined that Thomas had once again tricked me. By telling me to go ahead and investigate possible referrals, and to cover initial expenses, he was having me do his job. He, therefore, relieved himself of being obligated for that job at all.

That rationale allowed him to refuse to pay, since he did not do the work himself. He knew what he was doing. It was, in a way, cultural – the wording and verbal exchanges. But I believe Thomas knew full well what he was doing and that he would get out of paying for anything. This was a learning experience for me. I was truly learning how naïve I was, and how being so trusting was not necessarily a virtue.

This latest learning experience cost me more than $2,000, as Thomas refused to pay for the investigation, paperwork and travel expenses. Really, the only expenses left were court fees and travel fees for the children and social worker. At some point, Thomas had agreed to pay my guest house fees, but I was already paid up until November, so I didn't bring that up yet.

Roger estimated the following expenses:

Foster program fee (for paperwork and processing)	$1,000
Miscellaneous paperwork	$200
Investigation on background of both kids	$400
Ads in paper and on radio for Sasha	$200

Roger's fee	$1,500
Foster care fee	$500
Probation report fee	$300
Transportation	To be totaled
Witnesses to court	To be determined
Guest house fees (Discounted for me for long-term stay)	$620/month

So far, I was paying all this out of pocket, as Thomas refused to pay any of it.

Now began the waiting game. I decided not to bring the children to stay with me until right before court. I didn't want to have them with me too soon before court in case things fell through. Secondly, the added cost of having them with me was something I needed to prolong until I knew we would be leaving soon. So I waited….

In the meantime, I made lifelong friends with families at the guest house, spending time chatting, playing with kids, drinking wine on the balcony at night, playing cards, and watching movies after the children were all asleep. Mary and I were even invited to Roger's college graduation party at his house. We went shopping the day before with Charles, who took us to some fun markets (not tourist) and street shops. Mary bought a black dress, and I bought a long white skirt with black and orange flowers.

The day of the graduation was also the day of a soccer match in Kampala and, on top of that, it stormed all afternoon. Roger had said he would pick us up and take us to his party at his house and, surprisingly, he was four hours late. But as we were learning, this was "African time." Driving through Kampala was crazy with everyone celebrating the Ugandan Cranes' victory (the national football/soccer team). Roger lived quite a distance from town and, by the time we arrived, it was dark.

Ugandan graduation parties are interesting. There was a tent set up with rows of plastic chairs facing the front porch of the house. On the porch was a couch and more plastic chairs. As guests started to arrive, they took their seats under the tent. Mary and I were the only white people there. There was an emcee with a microphone who ran the party, which was for both Roger and a few friends who also had graduated. Roger's parents sat on the porch and faced us. At some point, we were ushered through a line at a table where we were given a plate with goat meat, matoke (a type of unsweet banana steamed and served like mashed potatoes) and greens and g-nut sauce (ground nuts cooked and blended like a sauce).

After the toasts and speeches, it was time to accept gifts. The graduates stood by the house, and the guests formed a line. The emcee was loudly introducing people who were handing out gifts and hugging the graduates. Mary and I were totally embarrassed and had no clue, but we got into line with our gift bag, which held a picture frame and watch for Roger. The emcee was still loud, and there was music playing over the speakers.

The line moved quickly, so we felt confident that we could casually hand Roger our gift and walk back to our seats. Not so! As soon as we reached Roger, everything stopped! The line stopped moving, the music and the emcee were all silent. All eyes were on us as we handed our gifts to Roger, and I gave him an awkward hug. Guests made us pose for a picture with Roger, then we scuttled back to our seats. We had a good laugh later, but it was so embarrassing at the time.

As we neared Thanksgiving, Mary got the good news that after more than five months, she and her girls would be going home. Families began to rotate through the house, all with different stresses and frustrations with the process. Jack and Connie, Grace and the staff were invaluable sources of advice, prayer and support. They became such good friends of mine, and I enjoyed their company at the house or on outings. I was happy for Mary, but my spirit was low because I was losing my closest friend there. I went with my friend and driver, Henry, to take her and the girls to the airport in Entebbe.

When it was time for them to go through security, I gave them hugs, trying not to cry. Mary's older daughter gave me a hug and told me she loved me. I think my heart burst for a bit there, missing them but loving them, and thankful for the time spent with them. I was also grateful for the love of these girls who encouraged me to hang in there, hoping for the day when I would be heading home with my own children.

Thankfully, I made many more friends, such as Natassia and Joe, who were adopting twin babies. When Joe had to return home for work, Laura, Natassia's mother, came to stay. We had a lot of wonderful nights hanging out on the balcony, sharing a bottle of wine, talking about everything in life and laughing a lot. There were many hellos and goodbyes as families came and went while I was waiting.

Thomas kept saying that he was applying for court, but then he would come up with another document or paper needed from Roger. Time was going by, and I still had no court date. It was obvious that since I was no longer paying Thomas, I was not his priority at all. I was trying to remain positive, but it was becoming clear that I was not going to get home for Christmas. I was hoping to have the court date any time, but even if court were in early December, all the government offices closed from December 15 through January 15, and I would not get a ruling or passports or International Organization for Migration (IOM) medical checks done in time to be home.

To keep myself busy, I decided to make stockings from African fabric for each of the staff and for Jack and Connie. The task kept me occupied, especially in the evenings. One afternoon, I was cutting out stockings in the dining room, and no one else was around. One of the Ugandan staff named Sarah came to talk with me. She is such a wonderful and amazing lady, and I am so blessed to call her my friend. After discussing the stockings and how I would still be in Uganda for Christmas, I think she could sense my struggle to be positive.

She told me she would pray for me. She said enough was enough and that surely God would give me the right kids this time. She told me to be patient, reminded me that Mary was there five months, but it all worked out all right. She said, "God's people must be patient." She said that He loves us and will honor that and give me my kids.

I knew as she was assuring me that the prayers I had been saying in my head over the last hour were heard and that God was speaking directly to me. I know that our God is always faithful. I reminded myself that I was not missing Christmas. The best present I could receive was to become a mother, and being in Uganda was an adventure. In fact, at some point in my younger life, I had prayed to God for an adventurous life. Although I realize that God does not always give us what we ask for, in some cases, as in mine, He gives it in spades!

Sometime later, as I was in town walking toward my lawyer's office from Barclay's Bank, a young man who was walking the same direction struck up a conversation with me. He was barely twenty years old, and somehow we got on the topic of photography. I was telling him how my sister and I did a lot of freelance photography on the side, shooting weddings and family portraits. He explained that he could use some help photographing his organization for its Facebook page.

His name was Joseph, and he ran a program for street kids. I took his contact information, explaining that I might be there for some time and would love to help take pictures. In a few months, this turned into a great opportunity.

In the meantime, I spent my first Thanksgiving in Africa! The food was made to comfort American families away from home. We had roast chicken from Jack and Connie's farm, plus mashed potatoes and steamed pumpkin. At the Shoprite grocery store, I found imported cheese from Europe. I bought brie, some pastry dough and orange marmalade. There is a brand of imported jam from Kenya that is amazing! It's red plum, which we had all the time at the guest house. I also loved the tropical fruit and orange marmalade. I baked the brie with the marmalade in the pastry dough as an appetizer with crackers. Abdul was one of the guests, and he loved it! I hadn't had much opportunity to cook at the house yet, so this was a fun opportunity. Renee made an apple dessert with Mountain Dew soft drink in it. It was delicious. It's funny that even far from home, familiar food can bring such comfort.

During my time in Uganda, I found places to get really good food. I didn't find the kind of variety that we have in the United States. In fact, I really began to realize how diverse America is and how many immigrants make up our culture. Not many countries have the variety of food and flavors we offer. As a result, many Americans enjoy a diversity of flavors. I found most of my Ugandan friends had a difficult time trying foods that tasted foreign to their culture.

In Kampala, I found local food to be similar tasting, using a seasoning called royco. For little money, I could go to a restaurant and order meat such as chicken, beef, goat or fish, which came in a tomato-based broth and was accompanied with choices of matoke, Irish potatoes, greens, sweet potato, cassava or, my favorite, steamed pumpkin. Matoke is a type of unsweet banana, which is cooked in a few ways, my favorite being similar to mashed potatoes.

On special occasions, I had luwombo, which is meat wrapped in banana leaves and cooked for hours. It is so good! If I bought dinner off the street, it most likely consisted of chips and chicken. The chicken is cooked in what we call rotisserie style and put into a plastic bag with shredded cabbage and sliced tomatoes. Chips are French fries that are handmade from potatoes and fried in oil over a small stove. I didn't care much for the most commonly found variety of ketchup, which was a bright neon red and tasted mostly of sugar and cornstarch. But I could find the Heinz brand at certain grocery stores.

Buying off the street, I also had beef on skewers and roasted bananas, but I never once bought food off the street by myself. My Ugandan friends always picked it out because they could choose the best places to stop and the best meat. I'm happy to say that I never got food poisoning, although I know many who did.

Transporting Sugar Cane

Oranges in the Market

Watermelon for Sale

I often went to one restaurant downtown Kampala called Diner's Choice. It was on the second floor of a building with shops and offices. The restaurant was basically a balcony where I could sit with friends and look over the busy traffic below. I still remember the giant billboard across the street advertising Sony cameras. Below were sidewalks, streets and, in the middle, a small park. I could sit for hours and watch the people.

My View from the Diner

Diner's Choice food was inexpensive. They served bottles of beer all day, and the owner was friendly. I often shared a plate of goat and chips or stir-fried chicken and masala chips. Stir-fried just meant it was sautéed. Masala chips were fries with a sauce of tomatoes and spices. At lunch they had a buffet of local dishes, which were inexpensive and good.

Another restaurant I frequented was called Sea Scallop. I had been there a few times with Henry and his friend Sande to enjoy juice or a beer. Uganda has the best juice! Passion juice was my favorite, and I could have drunk it every day. There was also mango juice, and watermelon juice or a combination. The Sea Scallop had a gym and sauna inside, as well as outside seating. This sounds strange to us, but it was common to combine businesses there. Eventually, I attended that gym frequently and would often get dinner there afterwards. I especially remember one night when the manager made me pork skewers that were perfectly cooked with roasted Irish potatoes, similar to potatoes we are used to.

Roadside Stand

Fish and Chips

Most food in Uganda is not produced on a large scale but, instead, comes from small farms. In fact, near the guest house I could walk and buy pineapples, sugar cane, mangos and more out of wheelbarrows. As far as I know, I was not eating any GMO (genetically modified organism) foods. Items such as tomatoes were so good that I ate them much more than I ever do at home.

I often treated my Ugandan friends to a meal at a restaurant like the Rancher's Steakhouse or the Terrace. The prices were so inexpensive by our standards, but not something they could afford. In June, I discovered that Kampala had a Restaurant Week. Participating restaurants advertised specials at a discounted price. I took two of my friends to a place called The Lawns. It was beautiful, looked like a safari lodge, all lit up at night, and open to the outside air.

We sat out under the stars on wicker patio furniture at a small table. There were pet bunnies running around that I got to pet. We ordered their special, which were skewers of various animals such as impala, gemsbok and kudu. We also ordered crocodile, which we all found to be disgusting! But I can say I've tried it. All those items were flown in from South Africa.

When I traveled outside of Kampala, I often found myself eating at small hole-in-the-wall places that had probably never served food to a white person. My friends always ordered for me. At one such place, I had matoke, rice, cooked cabbage and stewed beef in broth. It was very good and was accompanied by a bottle of Coke.

As we traveled along the roads, there might be a stretch of individual vendors grilling a variety of meats, frying chips, etc. A few places had umbrellas and plastic tables and chairs. We bought food, sat under the umbrellas and relaxed and enjoyed a beer. One such night, my friends picked out the best skewers of roasted goat meat, which were accompanied by plates of chopped onion and tomato. When we sat down, a waiter or waitress came with a basin of water and a bar of soap and held it while we washed up. Then we ate everything with our hands. After we ate, the staff returned with clean water so we could wash up again.

Most of my meals, however, were cooked by Grace, who was an

excellent cook. My two favorite things she prepared were fried plantains and her homemade donuts, which we ate hot, dusted in powdered sugar. Even now I'm melting thinking of them!

In my journal I noted this :

> *I have not acquired a taste for posho or the sweet potatoes here, which are white and grainy. I don't care for millet porridge, although I LOVE the corn porridge. I do not like papaya. I love mango when it's ripe, as well as pineapple. I accidentally ate liver the other day. Thought it tasted like canned dog food.*

Thanksgiving came and went with still no court date. As we neared Christmas, Connie let us help decorate a small fake tree and hang tissue paper flowers from the ceiling of the dining hall. My favorite coffee shop, 1000 Cups coffee shop in downtown Kampala, was playing Christmas music, the stores had toys everywhere, and it was fun to see how another culture celebrated in ways both similar and different from ours.

One day Renee, another adopting mother at the guest house, and I hired Charles to drive us to a Christmas market downtown. There was an empty lot set up with tents, and hawkers everywhere sold crafts, handmade jewelry, chess sets, baskets, clothing and trinkets. Much of it was imported from Kenya, with some local crafts as well. It was a fun way to pass the time. Renee was trying to find a keychain for her daughter and I was hanging out at the edge of the tent, just observing when, out of the sky, an orange fell on my head. I was mystified! I stood there looking at the sky, the tent tops, the tree branches overhead, trying to figure where in the world an orange came from.

Suddenly, I heard laughter nearby. I looked as a Ugandan woman in traditional dress was bent over laughing, with the basket of oranges she had been carrying now lying at her feet. Many Ugandans carry goods of all sorts in baskets on their head. As she walked by me, and because she was considerably taller than I am, an orange had accidentally tipped out and fallen on me. I couldn't help but share in the joke – how the clueless muzungu (white woman) thought oranges fell from heaven. I truly love Ugandans and especially their sense of humor.

Market in Kampala

Woman Selling Jackfruit

On December 4, my attorney e-mailed me late in the day saying that he needed more probation reports from Roger and that Roger needed to interview the director of the foster program. I had little hope of Thomas filing for court before December 15 at this point.

I wrote the following in a journal:

> *I feel desperate to get a court date in December and, yet, the days are passing, It feels like I am moving back and not forward. Lying in bed, I feel like I'm drifting in the ocean, getting beaten on the rocks, with a lighthouse in the far distance. It feels like I have to stop struggling and just float and crash where the waves will take me. I have no control.*

But friends had ways of lifting my spirits. A friend from home e-mailed me Psalm 63. I was especially moved by verses 6-8:

On my bed I remember you;
I think of you through the watches of the night.
Because you are my help,
I sing in the shadow of your wings.
I cling to you;
your right hand upholds me.

My friend Henry texted me, "Just know that God is in control; victory is around the corner." Grace thanked me for being patient and not giving up. On Sunday, December 7, Jack and Connie took me to church with them, and I wrote two things that helped get me through the week.

1. God is not limited by our fear.
2. If we are faithful to God in the small things, He will put us in charge of the big things.

I took courage in the hope that I was doing right—what was being asked of me for the sake of these children—and I would gain so much reward in being a mother!

I had many moments of loneliness and moments of doubt and despair. Even now. I know that without the prayers and encouragement of my friends there, and especially Jack and Connie, I would not have made it. Furthermore, although my last two attempts at adoption had failed and I had been deceived, I still had so much to be thankful for—most especially for the friendships I made with Ugandans.

Anywhere in the world there is evil and corruption and people take advantage. But I have never found myself so accepted and included and loved as I was by many of my new Ugandan friends. I will forever be grateful and cherish my friends.

My Lovely Friend Sarah

My Sweet Friend Fatuma

One very hot December Sunday, some of the girls who worked in the house asked me to go for a walk with them. They wanted to show me their homes and meet their families. The plan was to go by a few homes that day and visit some others the next week. I was honored to be asked. It was hot and dry, and we walked for about an hour. For some reason, I was especially exhausted that night. I assumed I had just gotten overheated. But in the middle of the night, I woke with sharp pains in my stomach, aching muscles, and I had to run to the bathroom to throw up. The next morning, Jack dropped me at the nearby clinic to get tested. After lab blood test results came back, the doctor informed me I had a bacterial infection. Most likely I had not gotten rid of the one I'd had in late October, and it had come back with a vengeance.

I was just thankful it wasn't malaria, as I had stopped taking my malaria medicine. Armed with antibiotics, I returned to the guest house, weak but relieved. The whole time I was in Africa, I was so blessed. Other than a few small cold viruses, the worst I faced was a recurring bacterial infection. All my family and friends in America were concerned because of Ebola, which, I believe, the media helped feed. In East Africa (note that the Ebola virus was in West Africa), there were signs posted to remind people to limit shaking hands, to avoid other contact, and to wash hands constantly.

Personnel at the airport had taken our temperature when we entered the country but, other than that, there was no fear or panic in Uganda concerning Ebola. There was a typhoid outbreak in Kampala that killed about 30 people, mostly young men. I learned that they were dying from dehydration because of typhoid contracted from a certain area. For that time, everyone was cautioned not to buy juice off the street, which is sold in plastic bags.

The clinics and hospitals surprised me. I had expected more primitive resources and, therefore, not much in the way of medical care. But the efficiency and skill of the doctors and lab technicians was fantastic. Furthermore, they were quick about obtaining results and seeing patients. The costs were incredibly affordable, compared to what we are used to in the United States. Seeing a doctor, having blood drawn and lab results obtained, and given antibiotics was about a two-hour wait and cost around 100,000 shillings (about $30).

Unfortunately, health care for Ugandans is still out of reach because of their average income, and many of my friends did not go to doctors until they were very sick. Most just visited the pharmacies. Pharmacies are everywhere and sell basic toiletries and medication. No prescription is necessary. Just ask for anything, including narcotics. Most drugs are generics from the Middle East. If you cannot afford a doctor, you describe your symptoms to the pharmacist, and he decides what you need.

Before I knew it, Christmas was upon us, and my lawyer still thought he could file for court and have a date for me soon after the New Year. I didn't believe him, as I knew government offices closed until January 15. I also found out that after the new year, judges were all at a conference until the end of January.

But since I was in Uganda, and the price of a plane ticket home and then another back was more than the cost of staying, I decided to enjoy Christmas. On Christmas Eve, I went with Jack and Connie to their farm just outside Kampala. My friend Abdul (who helped me with Anna and Benjamin), his wife and kids all lived on the farm and managed it. We took gifts for his kids. His five-year-old daughter loved the baby doll I gave her and, apparently, immediately told her mom that she needed to find her Pampers so she wouldn't wet the bed. Too cute!

My friends Mark and Renee gave me a journal as a present to encourage me to write this book. My first entry briefly described Christmas Day.

Dec. 25, 2014

Kampala, Uganda

> *I just returned from church with Jack and Connie. It was beautifully decorated with gold and green fabric streamers and Christmas lights. The service was beautiful. The Vicar spoke of the dirty manger stable where Jesus was born. But that is why we need Jesus. Our hearts are like the manger, and He purifies and cleans our hearts and makes us new.*
>
> *There were thunderstorms at 4:30 this morning, making it a cool and rainy day, which is unusual for this time of year in Uganda. There is not much traffic out. Everyone I see is dressed up and looking their best.*
>
> *Mark and Renee gave me this journal to write my book in, which is so awesome. Connie gave me an adorable hand-beaded clutch purse.*

Christmas in Africa!

With Natassia and Renee Making Cookies

My Bedroom View

Mark and Renee flew home with their son, Ian, that day. Natassia and the twins were already gone. There were not many families left at the guest house, and I was not as close with those who remained. I enjoyed Skyping with my family that afternoon. My brother lives in Cancun, so we did a three-way Skype with him in Mexico, me in Africa, and my mom, sister, grandfather and husband in Indiana. My mom and sister had saved a few gifts to open on Skype so we could see and be part of Christmas.

But as they went to get the gifts, I heard my mom yelling my dog, Murphy's, name. It seems that as we were chatting on Skype, Murphy ran to the tree, grabbed gifts and unwrapped them. I created a monster when I taught my dog to unwrap presents. I had to laugh. Things at home had not changed much.

December 26 is Boxing Day. I learned that Ugandans open gifts (if they have them) on that day. I also learned from Sharifah, one of the girls working at the house, that you should eat pork on December 23, you should eat beef on December 24, and you should eat chicken on December 25. Jack and Connie decided we should take a holiday, and we drove to Entebbe to visit the botanical gardens. It was beautiful. Entebbe is different from Kampala. It seems cleaner, greener and has more landscaping. There are also less-visible slums.

Entebbe is on Lake Victoria, and there are many hotels and tourist spots. I spent many evenings with Ugandan friends, hanging out at little places on the beach, listening to music, having a beer, playing chess, and eating grilled fish with our fingers. I will always love Entebbe. The botanical gardens are no exception. I assume it must be a botanist's dream. The trees tower to the sky with climbing vines and flowers. I saw trumpet flowers, which are deadly poisonous if eaten. I saw a parasitic tree, which somehow wraps itself around another tree.

I was told that the original black-and-white "Tarzan" movies were filmed here. I saw many types of birds, including fish eagles, kingfishers and the national bird, the Crested Crane. There are many types of monkeys that live in the gardens, including a troop of the black and white colobus monkeys. I had such a restful day exploring with Jack and Connie. We ended the evening by having Indian food at a restaurant on a hill overlooking Lake Victoria and the airport. Then we capped the day off with coffee at another restaurant. I was truly blessed with such good friends!

Colobus Monkey

Crested Cranes

Botanical Gardens in Entebbe

Vervet Monkey

Shortly after Christmas, two things happened. I met two documentary filmmakers and struck up a lifelong friendship. Also, my Uncle Gary and cousin, Aaron, arrived in Kampala to work with their non-profit organization.

The filmmakers whom I met are Emmanuel Tumuhairwe, Henry's cousin, and his business partner and roommate, Collin Mayambala. I have been so incredibly blessed by their friendship. They accepted me into their families and circle of friends, helping me navigate in a foreign culture for so long, challenging my narrow-minded views on the world, and inspiring my creativity.

Emmanuel and Collin

Filming an Introduction

Matts

I had been in touch with Joseph, the young man I met who ran a street kid program. He asked me to visit his program and meet the boys he was working with. Emmanuel drove me and stayed while I met all the boys being housed by Joseph's program. After that first meeting and talking with Emmanuel and Collin, we decided to do a short documentary film on street kids. A friend from home sent me a book on writing scripts for documentary films. So I did my homework, wrote an outline and submitted it to Collin.

Visiting Street Kids Program

I had met a woman in Indiana named Amanda, who was also in Kampala running a home for street kids. I contacted her, and she introduced me to Steven, a Ugandan social worker, who oversaw another program for street kids. With these three programs, we began filming and, over the course of the next four months, we filmed the programs, the kids in the slums, the conditions they lived in, the success of getting them off the streets – and the heartbreaking struggles.

From my journal:

February 18, 2015

> *I'm filming street kids today. Second time filming with Joseph and Simon's group. I LOVE filming. It's hot and tiring, and I don't even touch a camera. But last week with*

> *Steven and Amanda's group, I did five interviews. I loved*
> *every minute! These street kids will break your heart, they*
> *will make you love them, they will inspire you, frustrate*
> *you, and make you want to take them home. Oh, my heart.*
> *They are so lost in such a big world that is consumed with*
> *itself. I want this documentary to inspire people to think*
> *outside themselves, to see the world as it is – full of beauty*
> *and compassion, but lost in pain and suffering.*

I enjoyed every minute of it, and I truly hope I get to work on more documentaries in the future. The friendships I made along the way have changed my life. I am currently helping Joseph go back to school, as he was a street kid himself and never finished high school. The hope is to empower him with the education and knowledge to create change.

As of this writing, our documentary is in the final stages of being completed, and I hope to publish it on social media. My goal is to educate, to show the face of real street kids so viewers see and understand that these are not actors in a public service announcement on television. Like many Americans, I, too, had been sheltered and had never witnessed the truth.

The second event that happened after Christmas was the arrival of my relatives. I was overjoyed to see family! Henry was my Uncle Gary's driver the entire time he was in-country, and they regularly included me in their activities. It was the first time I was really able to get to know my cousin Aaron. Ironically, it had to happen on the other side of the world. My uncle and cousin own and run a plastics company in Indiana. As an offshoot, they are starting a non-profit company. The goal is to help young businessmen and women who have a promising business or idea, and whose main goal is to serve Christ and further His kingdom.

My uncle is a very wise businessman and such a faithful follower of Christ. Watching his excitement and passion in working with Ugandan businessmen and women was inspiring. He worked especially closely with Scripture Union and had previously come to Uganda to start a chicken farm on Scripture Union property to help make its children's camp sustainable. The farm had started with 4,000 chickens, but at this time were down to under 3,000. My uncle had consulted with a prominent specialist in the United States regarding large-scale chicken farms and had come with the desire to force the chickens to molt (shed old feathers and grow new ones). Forcing a molt in the proper way resets egg production and, ideally, increases it.

Chicken Farm

Scripture Union's chicken farm was located on Lake Victoria, close to Entebbe. The property is peaceful and beautiful. I had actually been there the week before Christmas with Henry for their camp Christmas party. The camp had a number of buildings, including one for activities, with a full kitchen in the back. There were also two sets of buildings to hold campers, complete with bunks and shower houses. When you first drive onto the property, there is a field of trellises laden with passion fruit. Behind the camp buildings are small structures for the family that lives there and helps maintain the property.

To the side of these are the chicken "houses." There is a long row of rectangular houses, four in total. At the end of the houses is a small area for grain and for sick chickens. At the end are the living quarters for the men working with the chickens. Behind the chicken houses, the land opens up to a few sparse trees and tall grasses, reaching a small hill that leads down to the beach of Lake Victoria. There are cattle and goats that roam the property, tended by neighboring farmers. On the beach are some fishing boats and birds of all kinds. I used to sit on large rocks at the edge of the water and listen to the waves and watch the birds and fishermen.

Fishing Boats

Lake Victoria

From my journal:
Winter 2015

> *Sometimes I can't believe this is my life. I'm a few days away from six months of being in Africa. I am sitting here under a tree looking out over Lake Victoria. To my left are some fishermen, a woman and a child who appear to be getting nets ready for the boat. To my right are the shallow waters. Among some tall grasses, two egrets are fishing.*

> *There is a warm breeze coming off the lake. I see at least four fishing boats, wooden boats reminiscent of canoes. Behind me on the hill lies a cow, relaxing in the shade, and on the other side of the hill, I can hear a few goats. It's peaceful here and quiet. I hear birds mostly. The yellow orb weavers, the funny greenish-brown birds with curved bills, the little finches and more. I can hear the waves lapping against a boat on shore. There are butterflies and millions of dragonflies with black-tipped wings fluttering around me. High above I hear a plane, perhaps on its way out of Entebbe Airport, flying to another exciting destination.*

Spending time with my uncle also afforded me the opportunity to travel to places I would not have been able to. He wanted to check into another organization that paired orphans with grandmothers. It was in Nasuti, which was a day's drive from Kampala. We stayed in a guest house owned by an American couple. It was (and still is) one of the most beautiful houses I have ever stayed in. I spent the day in villages, meeting these grandmothers and photographing the kids who ran to see the white people. It was a day of joy and happiness, even though we were in places of simple living and poverty. I fell in love with the children of Uganda all over again, and I do every time I look at their smiling faces.

My thirty-ninth birthday was January 5. My uncle and cousin planned the whole day off so that we could go on a safari! Jack drove us, and three of my friends came: Henry, Charles and Abdul. We left early, heading to Lake Mburo, which was four hours away. On the way, we stopped at a small restaurant on the Equator, had our picture taken, ate some samosas, then continued on our way.

It was a beautiful day, and I saw many animals, and even had a close encounter with a warthog. I saw antelope and water buffalo, and was especially excited to see zebras. We took a boat ride on Lake Mburo and saw hippos and a crocodile that was at least ten feet long! I saw monkeys and many birds. Not only was it a fantastic birthday, but it was also a day to delight in nature, relieve stress, and enjoy friends and family.

At the Equator with (standing) Henry, Uncle Gary
and Aaron and (kneeling) Abdul and Charles

Gazelle, Lake Mburo National Park

Zebra, Lake Mburo National Park

Warthogs, Lake Mburo National Park

Gazelle, Lake Mburo National Park

Water Buffalo, Lake Mburo National Park

Fish Eagle, Lake Mburo National Park

Fisherman on Lake Mburo

It was also a great day for my uncle to get to know Jack and Abdul, with whom he is now good friends. In fact, he was so impressed with Abdul that, after prayer and consideration, my uncle hired him to be the manager of the chicken farm. Abdul was placed in charge of the molting process of the chickens. My uncle also asked me, since I had the time, to work on the farm as well. For almost two months, I went to the chicken farm daily, catching chickens, weighing them, collecting eggs and supervising.

I loved having work to do, but also I loved working with animals. The work itself was truly a blessing. Witnessing Abdul's gift in managing a farm and turning it around was also inspiring.

One evening I was able to attend one of my uncle's business meetings in a very upscale Chinese restaurant. He was speaking to the group about how business was about people. God is interested in people. It reminded me that adoption is not about me, but about people. My adoption story was about Roberta and her children, James and Kira. It was about Leah and her children, Anna and Benjamin.

My story had now brought me to Paul and Sasha. My story was about Ugandans.

In January, I became brave and began riding bodas. A boda is basically a motorcycle taxi. You are the passenger and, for a very small negotiated fee, the driver will take you anywhere. Prior to my uncle's coming, I didn't have the nerve to ride one. The name "boda boda" is rumored to have come from the command "border border," as in "Drive me to the border." Most of the motorcycles are inexpensive bikes from India, which results in many boda drivers.

According to one statistic, there are 38,000 registered drivers in Kampala Central, and more than 120,000 without registration. (Nasasira, Roland. "The boda boda economy defining the streets of Kampala." *The Daily Monitor.* 15 September 2015. Web. July 2016. http://www.monitor.co.ug/Business/Prosper/boda-boda-economy-defining-streets-Kampala/688616-2869756-d4bwbo/index.html) You could pick up a boda driver at a "stage," which was a spot for boda drivers to park. Usually there is one man appointed as head of the stage and the drivers pay a small fee. The article cited above reports that there are about 5,000 stages in Kampala. I found that most drivers did not belong to a stage, but they drove around looking for hires.

Because I am white, and "white" is associated with having money, it was very easy for me to flag a driver. But it was important to get a good driver, since the streets were so congested and riding a boda can be very deadly. Grace, at the guest house, recommended a boda driver named Rajiib as one of the safest. I called him to pick me up at the guest house and drive me everywhere. Eventually, he even helped me purchase a helmet off the street.

Hiring a driver and a car to take me into town could cost me from 60,000 to 80,000 shillings (about $18-$25), whereas the same distance on a boda was closer to 5,000 shillings (less than $2) plus a tip. I know I paid a little more since I am white, and I think a Ugandan could have negotiated a ride into town for 2,000 shillings – less than $1.

Rajiib became a trusted friend whom I greatly admire and respect.

He was saving his money to buy a van, and he did before I left. I met his son, who was the sweetest little boy. Rajiib, like many of my friends, was a Muslim. Speaking for myself, as an American living a fairly insular life, I was not familiar with, nor had I ever met a Muslim. My time in Uganda opened my eyes and gave me a new respect for them. Rajiib is one of the most honest, trustworthy people I have known. I was blessed to have him as my driver while I was there, and for his friendship.

From my journal:

January 27, 2015

> *A few words about riding on bodas. Today was my most adventurous trip yet. Rajiib first took me to my lawyer's new office to sign affidavits. Of course, my lawyer didn't show up, although he said he'd be there. Anyhow, his new office is in Ntinda, which is quite far. Rajiib then took me to Watoto in Kampala. All the while I was holding a bag of three soccer balls and he had a bag of two soccer balls. I had my new backpack with my computer on my back. Yes, it was about an hour riding on a boda balancing myself and soccer balls.*

> *It's dry season, so the dust and heat is intense, but the worst is the exhaust from all the trucks. Sometimes going up a hill you ride through black clouds of exhaust, which obscure your vision. It's no wonder when I wash my hair at night the water turns brown!*

> *Riding a boda is being aware of your body, of balance and of the rhythm of the city. Start, stop, swerve, sometimes even back up to go around. I'm always amazed at the passengers who can talk on the phone while riding, or the women who sit sidesaddle because of their skirts. Some don't even hold on! I hold on tightly with my right hand on the grill behind me, to the point of my hand going numb.*

> *Rajiib is awesome. He speaks very good English and is*
> *an excellent driver. I always tip and pay him well, so he is*
> *sure to be safe, on time and available. He told me so! Today*
> *he was late meeting his family for a burial in the village*
> *because of driving me. I felt so bad, but he told me I have*
> *blessed him so he always wants to be able to take me.*

> *Boda drivers make so little money. Rajiib and I were*
> *discussing football today. He is a Manchester United Fan.*
> *He said he is going to miss me (my business) when I go.*

The funny part is that I wrote this in January. By the time I left in September, I was one of those who rode a boda while texting on my phone. I got so comfortable and used to riding them. But I never tried sideways like many women. I'm sure I would have fallen. I saw many accidents on bodas. I saw two men who were hit by a car, who were most likely killed. I saw an Indian woman riding, whose skirts got tangled in the wheel and the boda wiped out in the road. Thankfully, she and the driver were okay.

Many times if I was lonely or feeling homesick, I would take a boda into town and go to my favorite coffee house to order a mocha or passion fruit juice.When I was working at the chicken farm, I took a boda halfway there, and then Henry picked me up in a truck and drove the rest of the way. I saw so many things transported by bodas – goats, pigs, calves, puppies. Chickens would be hanging by the feet, tied to a stick and tied on the back. I saw as many people and children as could fit squished onto one boda. I saw coffins, keyboards, a mannequin, and other large items transported. It became so routine that it didn't surprise me anymore.

Boda Boda Passengers

Bodas in Kampala

Downtown Kampala Traffic

Even as I was beginning to enjoy everyday life in Kampala, I was increasingly frustrated with my lawyer and our lack of progress. In fact, my Uncle Gary was also beginning to voice his concerns to me. He had been discussing with Abdul and Jack what I had already gone through with my lawyer. They were of the opinion that my lawyer was doing nothing at all, hoping to prolong my stay and wear me down until I gave up and left.

Beth from Scripture Union set up a meeting about this issue with Mike Chibita. He is the Director of Public Prosecutions (DPP), appointed by President Museveni. He was at the top of their legal authority, the top judge. To have a meeting with him about my situation was unheard of.

Getting an hour of his time was an honor. I was very nervous! Uncle Gary, Abdul and Dickens, another Ugandan friend working with Scripture Union, went with me. I was apprehensive for a number of reasons. Not only was Mike Chibita a man of power and position, but the last time I had tried to get my lawyer Thomas to do something,

Thomas got very angry, and I had to apologize. But as Uncle Gary said, "You didn't set up this meeting." God took it out of my hands, so we went.

Henry knew Mike Chibita because Mike had worked with Scripture Union years ago. Henry encouraged me, saying that Mike is calm and easy to talk to. No one warned me how big he was! Abdul is a very tall, formidable man, but he was dwarfed by Mike, who had to be over 6' 4".

We met at Mike's office downtown, which was in a building called "The Worker's Place." It is a huge building, more modern and has tight security. His office was on the twelfth floor. My goal was to be confident, calm, assertive and not scared.

Dickens introduced us. Then I proceeded to tell my story, with Mike asking some questions. I tried not to be confrontational, but factual and to the point. Uncle Gary asked whether in Ugandan culture Thomas should have fired Jacob, the junior lawyer. Mike's answer was "no," since the police had not prosecuted Jacob, but were focusing on the pastor, so Jacob was "innocent until proven guilty."

Mike questioned whether or not I could still trust Thomas to work with him, or was it more because of finances and time that I needed to continue with Thomas. I answered it was the time and money invested, *not* trust.

Mike questioned Abdul, who also answered to the point. Abdul squarely put the blame on Thomas and also asked if we could prosecute my lawyer and the pastor from Benjamin and Anna's case. Mike said we should wait until the adoption was over or it would interfere. But we would prosecute and, as he stated, "Crime does not rot."

Before leaving, Mike assured me that he would get things moving and secure a court date for me.

It wasn't until February 5 that I heard that things were moving forward. Thomas contacted me to say that he had finally filed for court. He said Mike Chibita was taking over, and he hoped to secure a court date as soon as possible. It was clear from then on that my lawyer had very little affection for me and wanted to see me as little as possible. I'm sure he was shocked and somewhat afraid to learn I had connections "high up."

At that point, my emotions were running high, mostly from fear – fear of failure. I had failed two times already. Fear of Paul and Sasha not being my kids. I knew they were, but I still had fear. I was also afraid that I wasn't quite ready to leave Uganda yet. I was falling in love with the country, with the city of Kampala, with my friends. I had to prepare my mind that I might be leaving as soon as April. But I was praying that I could finish the projects I'd started before going. I was praying that I would leave when I was ready to go.

I had never lived in such a big city before. Furthermore, this was a city of noise and action, teeming with people, animals, pollution, and vehicles. I realized that being in such a place, a foreigner and alone, was a solitary feeling. For me, I often found a sense of peace and freedom in being surrounded by such chaos. I found myself feeling brave, adventurous and confident. These are characteristics I thought I had lost as I grew older.

Being alone in such a big city across the world from my home made me realize that the world is so enormous, comprised of so many strange and unfamiliar places and cultures. Yet, somehow, finding friends in such a place made me feel connected, helped me understand that God created us all in His image. I am still so humbled by my Ugandan friends. They gave me such acceptance and friendship and trust that I will always cherish.

I came across an African proverb that explained friendship to me: "If you want to go fast, go alone. If you want to go far, go together."

From my journal:

January 27, 2015

> *Right now my view from the diner overlooks a busy street. They are having a blood drive at the moment in the park down below. There is loud music and a man on a speaker calling people to come in the tent to give blood. At first, the city is so overwhelming. Many Americans are not used to the pace of the traffic and are easily put off by the*

noise, pollution of car exhaust, the trash and smells. It can all be intimidating.

But for now, I love it! There is always something new to see. It is such a radical mix of new and traditional. There are so many shops and people on the streets who sell everything you can imagine. There are women walking by in traditional dresses, and on their heads they are carrying baskets filled with fruit or other goods to sell.

Everyone is socializing. Occasionally, I get to watch boda boda drivers or taxi conductors get into fights. They are either trying to steal each others' customers or parking spots at the boda or taxi stages. So far, I've only seen half-hearted fighting, with the most physical being some pushing and shoving or slapping the side of a taxi.

Occasionally, when I get out of the city and into the villages, it's surprising to me. It's like not knowing you are thirsty and being given a glass of cold water. You suddenly realize how thirsty you were. I love the villages. The clean air, the quiet, the green. It's like a vacation.

But the truth is, I love Kampala. It fits me. It suits me for now.

While I waited for a court date, life at the guest house carried on as usual. In early February, Jack asked to speak to me. He had just had a meeting with Connie and Grace about a troubling e-mail they had received from one of their past guests. It turned out that an American adoption agency was sending out an e-mail to all its clients, telling them they were banning them from staying at Jack and Connie's guest house while they were in-country.

The agency claimed that there was an incident at the guest house where the police were called in the middle of the night and a questionable attorney and a babies' home (for infants and toddlers) were involved. They claimed it was not a safe place for families to stay during the adoption process, and it appeared that corrupt practices were happening.

I was furious. Jack and Connie had been so instrumental in guiding me to doing the right thing. They had helped me navigate corruption and reunite children with mothers. They were such sincere Godly people who cared so much about each one of their guests. They cried with us when things went wrong, advised us, rejoiced with us. This was their business, their home and their ministry.

For this agency to use my situation, and use it so incorrectly, was absurd. It also showed the huge lack of information that American agencies had on what was happening in-country. I truly believe this agency was just the norm. They tried to control their clients with the little information they had. One bad case could ruin their reputation and cost them clients and money.

I wrote a reply, which Jack and Connie approved before I sent it.

> *My name is Christine. I was disturbed to read your memo regarding Connie and Jack's guest house. I am staying there for the second time, and I have currently been here over 4½ months.*
>
> *The "case" you were referring to with the police coming at night is my case. But, unfortunately, you did NOT have the facts and you jumped to a very harmful conclusion. As you are surely aware, there is a lot of corruption in adoption. I have dealt with it here AND with American agencies.*
>
> *Recently, I was in a situation where God guided me to reunite two children with their mother. With Jack and Connie's wisdom, guidance, prayer and support, I was able to protect two children from an unfortunate circumstance, and we had their mother escorted by police for her safety in coming to get them.*

*The facts in your memo were false and unfortunate.
I fear you might be doing more harm than any good.
Anyone who has stayed at this guest house can attest to the
integrity, love and support shown to adopting families. This
guest house is run as a ministry and has blessed all who
stay here. Please, PLEASE get your facts right and speak
to people who have actually stayed here before you publish
such harmful misinformation.*

*In ALL aspects of adoption, as an adopting family
AND as an agency, we need to be ACCOUNTABLE for
all our actions and words.*

*Thank you,
Christine*

I received an apology from the agency, and they said they were correcting the mistake. It was not the first, nor the last, time I heard or saw such misinformation and false practices circulate from American agencies. The longer I remained at the guest house and got to know adopting families and hear their stories and frustrations with the process, the more I came to understand that no matter what anyone claims, adoption is a business.

It is not a charity or a ministry. Frankly, it is big money. It is my responsibility, as the adopting family, to make sure that what they are doing is ethical and in the best interest of the child and of the child's family. It is my responsibility to know if what I am doing is right. I was naïve to think that an agency is trustworthy. They have a bottom line to meet and employees to pay. They are so far removed from the country they are working with. They do not see the whole picture. They are making a lot of money and have a lot at stake if they lose their reputation.

As I was waiting to continue my adoption process, my uncle returned to Kampala for a couple of weeks at the end of February.

From my journal:
March 2, 2015

Yesterday, Henry, Uncle Gary and I picked up Ruth in Kampala and drove to Kassanda to spend a few hours with Paul and Sasha. When we arrived in Kassanda, the kids were in church, and Pastor Luke wanted me to greet the church.

It was a wooden building, almost like a barn. The walls and roof were wide slats that let the light shine in. People sat on wooden benches placed in rows on the dirt floor. It was beautiful in a simple way. There were twenty to thirty people. The women did African ululating (a long wavering high-pitched vocal) of celebration when I walked in. Across the room, Sasha saw me come in and ran to me. Everyone cheered. It melted my heart!

I knew that Pastor Luke and Ruth said the kids had missed me, but I'd only met them once for an hour in October. I didn't realize how well Pastor Luke and Ruth were doing in letting the kids know about me.

We took the kids to the foster program office with Ruth, where we played with them for an hour and a half. I had bought some toys at the U.S. Embassy supermarket. For Paul, a semi-trailer truck with three small cars from the Disney movie "Cars" and some plastic jungle animals. For Sasha, I bought two small baby princess dolls. I also brought a plastic ball I'd had for them since Christmas.

Paul played with the truck for a little while, then spent the next hour playing ball with Uncle Gary. Sasha sat in my lap, playing with the dolls and jungle animals. I also gave them each a new set of clothes and shoes: sandals for

Paul, who had feet the same size as mine, and little flip flops for Sasha. Oh, my goodness, did she ever go crazy over those shoes! She LOVED them! She even said (translated by Ruth) that she couldn't wear them outside or someone would take them.

Sasha was so happy. She was talking to herself and singing, while running in and out of the office, laughing. Ruth began laughing at one point, saying that Sasha was singing her own song, "Who do these belong to? They belong to me." She reminds me of my sister, singing and making up her own songs.

Paul is quieter, but he smiles and laughs and loves football (soccer). He is observant and great at sharing. If Sasha takes something, he lets her, without any complaint. He walked up to Uncle Gary at one point and brushed grass off his back. He is just the sweetest kid. I love them both already and can see they are mine.

When we dropped them off later with their Aunt Kate, Sasha cried, and they had to carry her off.

These visits helped keep me excited and motivated to be their mother.

Meanwhile, by March 10, Thomas claimed he had filed for court. Mike Chibita was contacting me for the case number it was filed under. Thomas assured me that he was keeping in contact with Mike and would text him the case number. I did not trust him at all at this point, but it was beginning to feel like things were moving along.

After seeing Paul and Sasha again, I had mixed feelings. I loved the kids and wanted them to be mine, but I was scared to go through the process again and possibly fail. I was also not yet ready to face leaving Uganda. I was working daily at the chicken farm for my uncle and was finishing up filming the documentary with Collin and Emmanual. I had many friends and was keeping myself busy. There was a freedom and a joy in finding a place to fit in.

As it turned out, I still had time. Mike Chibita informed me that court was scheduled for May 12, but then I got a notice from Thomas's office that court was moved to May 26. However, in early May, I got an e-mail from Thomas saying that he needed a copy of my entry visa to request a sooner court date. Since court was only weeks away, I found this odd, so I contacted Thomas.

He was surprised by my question and said, "Whoever said court was May 26? Court is August 26!" I was suspicious. How could he pretend I never even had a May court date when Mike Chibita knew I had a date. I felt like there was a trick behind this – more games, more annoyance. I contacted Mike Chibita who said he would work on getting me a sooner date. Again!

In the middle of May, I made another day trip to see Paul and Sasha. This time, my friends Emmanual and Matts and Robert (Emmanual's brother) came with me. We picked up Ruth, the social worker, and stopped in Mubende for lunch on the way. We arrived early afternoon and sat under the trees outside Kate's small house.

I held Sasha, and the guys kicked a ball around with Paul for a little while. It was a short visit, but it was so good to see the kids again. Upon leaving the village, I stopped and bought food and toiletries and had them sent back to Kate. I was nervous thinking that soon I would have complete care of these little ones. But having my friends by my side gave me confidence.

In the meantime, I began looking for a less expensive place to stay. I decided that if I rented my own house or apartment, I could save money, especially since having the kids with me would increase my fee at the guest house. My friends Rajiib and Charles began looking for a place for me to rent, driving me to different places. This was such a different experience, looking for a rental in a different country. I knew that the most important thing would be to find a place that was comfortable and where I felt safe. My friends even showed me a few apartments on the opposite side of Kampala. I looked at everything from shared houses near the guest house, to apartments near the embassy, near downtown, outside of town, and near the slums.

Timothy, a young Ugandan medical student who came to the guest house frequently to help prescribe medications, heard I was looking, and he knew of a house nearby for rent. It was about twenty-five minutes walking distance from the guest house; therefore, it was in an area I knew very well. It was in a gated compound with a guard. There was a large apartment building with rooms for rent or a small two-bedroom house where the landlady, Doreen, and her sister, Esther, stayed.

I found that I could rent this house with two bedrooms, a sitting room, bathroom with shower, and small kitchen for three months at the cost of one month at the guest house. I knew I could save money on food. I loved the guest house and firmly believe that the time and money spent there was worth every penny. I would not have had the courage or knowledge about how to live on my own if I hadn't spent the time there. Thankfully, Jack and Connie understood and supported my decision and told me to come and visit with the kids any time.

After packing all my stuff into bags, my friend Rajiib, (the boda driver, who now had saved enough money and had purchased a van!) picked me up and drove me the few minutes it took to get to my new place. There was actually a TV with a DVD player and, after not having watched TV for months, this was actually an adjustment. But I did enjoy having some noise in the place. After living in the guest house surrounded by other children and families, it was too quiet.

Eggs, Airtime, and Chapati for Sale

Neighborhood Store

Local Shopping

I still met regularly for coffee with some of the guest house families. There were two men at the guest house, Mike and John, each adopting little girls. Their wives were back in the United States for one reason or another. I have HUGE respect for these men who navigated so much of the adoption process in-country, alone, while bonding with and caring for little girls. I enjoyed meeting them for coffee, riding on bodas, shopping for shoes at the Oweno market or shopping for gifts at the Friday markets.

Both families had problems once they got to the U.S. Embassy, and I could see their frustration and stress, but they were amazing. Mike finally got his visas and he and his daughter left for home. John, on the other hand, did not have such good luck, and his case had to be sent to the U.S. Embassy in Rome. He had to return to the United States to work and had to leave his little daughter in the care of a Ugandan family.

I saw the anguish this caused and the fear that all the trust that he had built with this little girl would disappear. I gladly agreed to go and visit their daughter frequently and check on her, taking pictures and video to send him, and taking her gifts and showing her pictures of her dad and mom. I was thankful to be able to help and, even now, I feel fond and protective of this girl. I was so excited when they got approval and both John and his wife, Brooke, came to take her home. They asked me to go with them to pick her up, and I got to spend some time with them before they returned home.

It was hard, always being alone and left behind, but I am so thankful for the friendships and experiences I had. These children are so incredibly precious, and I love them so much.

Soon everything was to change.

I was under the impression from my lawyer that I now had a court date in late August. But in mid-June, I received a phone call from Beth telling me that I needed to check my e-mail for an urgent message from Mike Chibita about court being moved up to next week. I remember getting that call and my emotions ranged between wanting to throw up and wanting to pass out. I don't know why.

When Beth called, I had been lying on my bed in tears, feeling alone and frustrated. I had so many good friends in Uganda, so it wasn't for lack of care or friendship. It was just a feeling of not knowing what I was doing. Things were taking so long, and I no longer felt confident in the process. Furthermore, although I thought I had made it through the previous trial with few repercussions, now I knew that I was wrong. I felt dread and panic at the thought of going through this again – and this time alone.

Court was scheduled for a Monday at 9 a.m. I contacted my lawyer immediately, and he confirmed that we did have court, and that the date and time had been secured by Mike Chibita. My lawyer said he would work with Roger, the social worker, to arrange travel for the children, the witnesses and the other social worker, Ruth.

I arranged for them to come on Sunday because I didn't want to have the kids with me too long before court. I remembered what had happened the previous time. I assumed that if it was made clear that I would not succeed at Legal Guardianship, I would find it out in court.

I was a mess that weekend; my nerves were on edge. I spent the weekend with friends, who assured me that this was what I'd been waiting for, this was the purpose, and it would be fine. I just needed courage. On Sunday, I began getting frantic messages and calls from my lawyer and the social workers, Roger and Ruth.

Roger and my lawyer were arguing over the cost of travel and accommodations for everyone. The travel party included Ruth, Kate, an aunt Patricia, and two uncles, as well as the two children who were supposed to stay with me that night. Roger claimed he needed 500,000 shillings (about $150), and my lawyer only agreed to 300,000 shillings (about $90).

Neither Roger nor my lawyer would cooperate with the other, so I had to wire Roger an extra 100,000 shillings ($30). Because of their arguments, the delay caused them to get in late that night, and Roger decided they should all stay at his house, and I would meet them in the morning at court.

Of course, in the morning, I was a nervous wreck, but I had a driver coming early. Unfortunately, traffic was awful and, even leaving an hour early, I was almost late and had to take a boda to arrive at court to meet my lawyer. The kids and relatives all arrived late and we stayed in the waiting room together. I remember going down the hall to the bathroom to try to calm down. My friends were calling and texting me. They had even offered to come to court and support me if I needed. They assured me I could do this.

After waiting 30 minutes or so, someone informed my lawyer that the judge was out of town and had rescheduled our court session for the next day at the same time.

Thomas refused to provide any more money for the witnesses' accommodations, so I had to give Roger another 200,000 shillings ($60). Now Roger had a total of 600,000 shillings ($180), and I was told later he gave Ruth only 200,000 shillings to pay for their travel, food and accommodations – and pocketed the rest.

I called Rajiib to come and pick up the kids and me. We immediately went to Game (a small department store) and Shoprite (a grocery) to get some food. Then I remembered that when we left court, the aunt said something to Ruth to pass along to me, which was that Paul gets car sick. Ha! But, thankfully, that day both kids just slept in the van.

I remember that at Shoprite I had to watch Paul closely. He wanted to push the cart, and he almost ran into other shoppers because he was going too fast. He also kept putting things into my cart, which I had to take out and put back. I knew that he and Sasha were excited, since they had most likely never been in a big city, maybe never in a van, and probably never in a large store. Everything was new to them and, although I was terrified, I imagined they also were scared.

I don't even remember the rest of the day. I think I tried cooking dinner for them – and they didn't like it. The next morning, we got up early again for round two at court. I made them oatmeal, which made Sasha cry, and Paul took one bite and said "NO!" very loudly. I had nothing else made for breakfast. I assumed they would eat oatmeal, since the kids at the guest house ate it, and it was similar to porridge. Boy, was I wrong. I ended up eating some of it, and then we were on our way to court.

Here is my journal entry while waiting at court.

June 23, 2015

> *Waiting room of Crusader's House, which is where court takes place. We came yesterday, but the judge was in Mubende, so the clerk told us to come today at 9 a.m.. It's now 9:11 a.m. and the judge is not here yet.*

> *I got word about court last Tuesday. Beth called saying there was an urgent e-mail from Mike Chibita. So I am here and terrified. Yesterday the kids stayed with me at the rental house. They speak no English, and it was at moments ok, but mostly panic. Pure panic. If my friends hadn't kept checking on me, I would have been lost.*

> *Last night the kids went to bed around 7 p.m. and were asleep by 7:30 p.m. But they woke up at 3:30 a.m. to go to the bathroom. Then I couldn't fall back asleep. They woke again at 4:40, 5:00, and 5:30 a.m. They wanted to*

get dressed and go play. Finally they fell back asleep, but I was awake, and lack of sleep is equaling lack of courage.

I'm afraid I will not be a good mother, that I can't do this. But my friend told me to trust God. It has to move forward. So I have to breathe and believe that God knows better than I do what is best for these two.

This time the judge was there, and I remember Kate made me hold Sasha. I sat next to my lawyer, facing the judge. Courtrooms are very small, more like an oversized office. The lawyer and his assistant sat facing the judge, along with the kids and me. There was a microphone in front of me. I remembered that last time my lawyer was missing documents, so this time I brought all the papers I had. Of course, I forgot to bring my passport. Oh, well.

Sasha fell asleep in my lap, and she was sweating so much, as she always did while sleeping. I remember being embarrassed and annoyed because Kate kept giving me a handkerchief and motioning to me that I needed to wipe Sasha's forehead. I was already failing as a mother! I know this is ridiculous, considering the pressure I was under at the time, but such were the thoughts going through my head.

Paul was sitting next to me on my left. Behind me in a row of chairs, Ruth was sitting. To the left along the wall Kate, Patricia and the uncles were sitting. Also, the Local Council chairman arrived.

The judge started by asking the lawyer and Ruth questions. Then the judge, a woman, started with questions about Sasha. My lawyer and Ruth confirmed that Sasha was found outside a church in Kassanda where Kate worked, and she was abandoned. They took Sasha to the Local Council, who had them take her to the police, where a statement was made.

The appropriate steps where made to inquire if she had family. When I came into the picture, I paid for ads on the radio and in the paper with Sasha's photo to see if any family would claim her. No one had come forward, they said. I remember the judge asking how family would claim "Sasha" when that wasn't even her given name, when no one knew her given name, and it was the name that Kate had given her.

Next, the judge questioned Kate at length, first about Sasha, then about Paul. The judge asked Kate a lot of questions about her role in the foster care program. Questions regarding how many children she cared for, how much money she received in the program, where she worked, how much she was paid, if the house was part of the foster program, etc. Later I thought this might be a sign that the judge was leaning toward alternative care and not toward Legal Guardianship. I think that is what prompted all the questions, but I think judges still recognized that alternative care was not yet viable or preferred to Legal Guardianship.

Then the judge began to question Kate about Paul. What I remember most about this questioning is how confusing it was. After questioning Kate, she questioned both uncles. The second uncle was the younger one, and he was extremely nervous. He had to stand at a microphone next to me, and he was shaking. When the judge asked him about how he was related (and all this was translated to him from English to Luganda by the judge's clerk), he made the mistake of telling the judge that he was an only child. If he was Paul's uncle, how could he be an only child?

The judge started getting angry and, the more aggressive her questioning, the more nervous the uncle got. My lawyer kept saying that the man is insane, he's crazy, he doesn't know what he's saying. I was getting more and more upset because they were so cruel to this young man who was probably only twenty years old.

Finally, the judge was very upset when she began to question Paul. She asked Paul who the guy was and Paul said it was his brother. Now the judge was getting furious, since Paul was supposed to be an only child. Paul seemed confused, but they finally got him to say that the man was his uncle. They explained to the judge that Paul was just confused. She finally seemed satisfied and moved on to questioning me.

I remember she asked why my husband was not there. She said that was strange. She also asked why we had had so many different jobs over the years. She noted that I must really want children since the last two times we had tried to adopt, we had failed and I was still there almost a year later. She asked if I would be working or taking care of the kids. She also asked if I would hold it against Sasha since she was abandoned and would I treat her badly. She asked why I wanted two children and said that one was better. She also said that Paul should have another boy to play with, not Sasha.

After about two hours of being in court, we were finished, and the judge told my lawyer that she would have a ruling by the following Friday, which would be July 3. I had already found out that my case had been moved to criminal court, and I was one of the last, if not the last, case she would be hearing in family court. I also knew that family courts closed for vacation from July 15 through August 15.

Leaving court, my lawyer assured me that he felt it went well and I would most certainly get a favorable ruling for both children. He immediately left. Ruth wasn't sure how court went. She seemed a little nervous, but didn't say much one way or another. She needed to leave with the aunts and the uncles right away, and they seemed eager to get a taxi and go. I don't remember them even giving much attention to the kids.

We were standing outside the building in the parking lot, and Kate came and gave me a handshake. The aunt Patricia, who didn't speak much English, just came up to me and said, "Trust in Jesus." Then they were all gone.

Suddenly I was left with these two children—alone. I called Rajiib, and we stood on the sidewalk waiting for him. I remember being surprised that Sasha didn't cry and that both kids seemed brave. Everything was so new to them. Every time they saw a white person, they yelled "muzungu" and got my attention. An Indian man walked by us on the sidewalk, and Sasha ran up to him and grabbed his hand, which surprised him for sure! I was so nervous. The kids spoke no English at all. I felt lost and scared and alone.

That night, I cooked chicken and plain noodles, which they ate. I put the movie "Aladdin" on my computer, and then they were in bed early. Sasha was upset the next morning and cried a lot. Fred, the guard, told me she should go back to her mom. I tried to explain that she had been abandoned, and she didn't remember her mom.

So started the beginning of twelve very long weeks. Yet, looking back, it was such a blur. Now I can focus with a more critical eye on what happened. But at the time, those days and weeks were terrifying. The first three weeks, especially, I was a mess.

I was not confident, I was scared, and I didn't sleep or eat. It was as if I had never been around kids. My friends would stop by, and they could get the kids to behave. They were calm and confident, and I was a wreck, always on the verge of tears.

The first week we really did not leave the house much, although on that Thursday I hired a driver, and we went to Acacia Mall where I let them play in the indoor playground. We did the same again on Sunday. Then we met my friends Matts and Lues at Chili's Takeaway for dinner.

By this time, I knew that Sasha could have a tantrum over anything. I think it was the third night with me that I first saw this. Something upset her at bedtime, and she began to cry, really cry, sobbing. I held her for about an hour until she fell asleep. I remember messaging Ruth and telling her. She told me she would come the next week and check on us.

Once that week, I was taking a picture of the three of us and thinking that maybe I could do this. But at that time, I felt I could handle Sasha, but Paul was going to be more challenging. All the while, I was still hoping the judge would rule "no." I felt so much guilt over this and despised myself for being weak. For some reason, I had so much dread and fear and felt like this was all a mistake.

I remember I had heard from my husband only once that week, two days after court, asking how it had gone. At that time, he expressed his frustration and admitted that he wanted to quit the process months ago. At this point, I knew he was working long hours and overtime. I think the process had gone on so long that he was burned out. I now felt even more isolated and more alone.

The second week, things began to get more challenging. Sasha began to have more and more tantrums. Without being able to communicate with her in English, there was little I could do. When she got upset about anything, she cried, which turned to screaming. She lay on the ground, kicked and rolled around, and screamed. It got to the point where this happened constantly.

One day I think she did this every ten minutes. If she didn't like the dress I picked out, if Paul had a toy she wanted, if she didn't like the food, if Paul was sitting next to her, she threw a tantrum. The whole neighborhood knew we were there because she was screaming and crying at all hours.

My landlady, Doreen, and her sister, Esther, lived behind me, along with Fred, the guard. Sasha loved Fred because anytime she cried, he would hug or hold her, and he would yell at Paul. I was constantly asking Paul why she was crying, and he would shrug his shoulders, not knowing. If Sasha motioned that Paul had done something, I would ask him, and he would get wide-eyed and say "no!"

Esther and Doreen

Since Sasha cried and threw tantrums over everything, I began to think that she had abandonment issues. She also would go to anyone, and she didn't seem affected when she left Kate. For a few nights, she cried, wanting her mom, and I assumed she meant Kate. But other than that, she seemed not to miss anyone.

Here are my journal entries for those first few weeks.

July 14, 2015

Sasha's Tantrums: She throws tantrums when she doesn't want to pick up toys, she screams when I put her in bed, and she throws shoes at me. She spits on Paul. I tell her "no," and she throws a rock at him. She spits on Paul again. I tell her "no," and she throws a board at him. I lightly swatted her butt.

She eats all her chicken, wants Paul's chicken, throws a tantrum and tries to hit him. She wants Paul's toys, she doesn't like her dress, she wants an orange sweatshirt like Paul's, she doesn't want to wear a Pamper to bed. Who knows half the time?

She screams and kicks and cries, then runs out of the room laughing. Just now she was screaming, then stops and pretends to be chewing gum or something. She might be insane.

July 15, 2015

Nonstop screaming tantrums and now bad-tempered. She's been throwing things, spitting on Paul. She threw rocks at him. She threw her shoes at me. She just threw her backpack. Anything makes her mad.

I was going to send her back for a week, maybe for good. But Thomas said if I refuse to adopt her before the ruling comes out, I jeopardize getting Paul. I'm praying the ruling is a "no" for Sasha. I'm so worn out and sick of this that it's making me not want to be a mom at all.

July 21, 2015

> *Sasha threw at least two tantrums this morning, One didn't last long because she had food on her plate, and the other lasted only a minute or so because I ignored it.*

> *I realize I have disconnected. I feel guilty because Paul deserves more. But after four weeks of nonstop tantrums from Sasha, and Paul tattle-telling and neither one of them understanding me.... I don't deserve to be a mother. That vision I had of my kids is gone.*

> *Now it feels like waiting for judgment. The ruling will decide if I have to be a babysitter forever, or if I can rediscover my life.*

July 22, 2015

> *Still no ruling. Stress is like being on the edge of a cliff, waiting to step into nothing. I'm still hoping for a ruling of "no" – either for both or for Sasha. Some days or moments, I'm sure it will be a "no," and I'm already planning what I will do.*

> *Other days I panic and am sure I will get a call any minute that it's "yes" for both, and my life will be over.*

> *Then there is the guilt of having been here so long – having so many people say they are proud of me. I get this far and realize it's not what I want at all. I know the boredom (of the kids) and the language barrier are huge obstacles right now. But I feel it's more.*

Looking back at these journal entries makes more sense now. But at the time, I was so caught in despair and depression. The feeling of being such a complete failure was overwhelming. I'd waited a year and was such a fool thinking I could be a parent to two orphans. I'd disappointed myself so much, thinking I was a strong person, only to realize that I was completely self-centered and incapable of caring for a three- and five-year-old.

In the meantime, my husband (whom I hadn't heard from much because of his working overtime and being exhausted) was now telling me that he didn't have the energy to be a parent. I knew then that there was no way I could do this on my own. Sasha's tantrums were now every ten minutes or so. I could no longer take her anywhere. She and Paul couldn't get along at all; they fought nonstop.

I went and talked with Connie at the guest house. She agreed with me. She said that occasionally over the years she had seen a child with behavior like Sasha's being adopted, but it was always a case where only one child was being adopted and both parents were there supporting each other. She agreed that adopting a child with issues like Sasha's would put a lot of stress on a family that would already be stressed adopting another child.

So I contacted Ruth. Ruth had been visiting about once a week, which was unusual for a caseworker to do after court but, at the time, I was thankful. She knew and saw the trouble I was experiencing with Sasha. She had tried to talk with her and get her to behave. She even told me I had to listen to my heart, and she would understand if I sent Sasha back.

So when I made the decision and tried to send her back, it still took some time to coordinate. Ruth was in Kassanda and couldn't come right away. Pastor Luke was so upset with me. He was sending me messages on Facebook, wanting to have "an organizational meeting." I made it clear that I was not going to change my mind. Then he asked me to "have mercy" on a "needy child." He wanted me to support Sasha financially. But Ruth was telling me that Sasha would be adopted by another family right away.

I felt horrible and guilty and angry. I knew so many people, including my family, were going to be disappointed and angry with me. It was all up to me, and I was failing. I was now a quitter. I knew I was going to have to take responsibility for this, and I was miserable.

I have never in my life felt such despair and shame. Some of my Ugandan friends were supportive, and some thought I should have been able to handle it – that it was not such a big deal. I remember one Sunday late afternoon, when I had a rare moment out, while the kids were with a sitter. I rode past the Irish embassy. I suddenly realized that I could perhaps get a visa to Ireland and just disappear. It was a relief to dream of escape, but it added a huge weight of guilt, knowing that I shouldn't feel this way.

I "knew" that nobody adopting felt this way. All the other families were elated to get a favorable ruling and move on in the process. They couldn't wait to get home with their new family. Yet here I was, wishing simply to escape.

After having Sasha with me for five weeks, I arranged for Ruth to come and pick her up on a Sunday morning. The day before I had taken the kids to Bugolobi Village Mall to play in the indoor playground. It began well, but then Sasha threw a tantrum and ran away from me. I had to chase her down into the men's bathroom, while leaving Paul and my computer in the food court. The day went downhill from there.

The next morning, Sasha saw me packing all her stuff, and she knew she was leaving. When Ruth came, Sasha was very quiet but never cried. When I put her on the boda behind Jimmy, my boda driver, I cried – not because I was going to miss her, but because I felt so much pain for this little child who was so alone and angry and didn't even cry when she left. I was such a failure.

When I walked back to the house, Paul was running around back telling Doreen, the landlady, and Esther, her sister, and Fred, the guard, that Sasha was gone and it was going to be quiet. I knew that Paul and Sasha weren't related, and they had fought so much, but I was surprised that after living with her over a year with Kate, he wasn't sadder to see her go.

Even now, writing this two months after my return to the United States, I feel such overwhelming guilt and shame. At the time, I was in such a bleak place and felt like such a failure. There was so much despair and disappointment. Now I feel shame and guilt for not having been more understanding to Sasha, more sympathetic. I feel that I was so unhappy and stressed that I was selfishly deciding what I could and couldn't handle. Even knowing the truth and reality of the situation now, I will still carry the guilt of that experience and the shame of failing, and feelings that I don't deserve to be a parent.

My confidence is low enough now that I'm not sure I will ever feel that I deserve to be a parent. That is not an easy thing to admit to oneself.

I do want to say that there are three instances that I can look back and say that I saw Sasha's true personality. I pray that she gets the life she deserves, the stability she deserves, and whatever God has planned for her because her personality was simply awesome – if/when it gets a chance to shine through.

One instance was an afternoon when I was in my room on my computer, feeling particularly stressed and low, and she came into the doorway and did a little dance, made a face and ran away giggling. The second was when we were at the pharmacy and next door was a children's clothing boutique. Outside were two child-sized mannequins. Sasha walked up to one, shook its hand and said, "Jeebaleko Ssebo," which translates to "How do you do, sir?"

The third time I remember that I was lying on my bed with her, watching the movie, "Enchantment." If circumstances had been different, it would have been such a joy, such an honor to be her mother. She had so much personality. In a way, she was like me. She had so much anger and fear and was in such confusion and distress that her only outlet was tantrums.

Now I can hardly blame her. I'm sitting here writing this in a café, a world away and months after leaving Uganda. I have tears streaming down my face because now I can look back and feel her fear and anger and I wish so much that I could hold her and comfort her. But I was so boxed in by my own feelings that I missed the truth and the opportunity. I pray that God can heal her, release her anger, and let her know how amazing she is and that she deserves to be loved.

After Sasha left, the next week with Paul was easier in a way, but also confusing. I was confused because, quickly, his behavior changed. He went from this sweet boy who wanted to give me high fives and wanted hugs all the time, a boy who wanted to please me and be helpful, to a different child.

Suddenly, he disobeyed constantly, argued (albeit in another language) all the time, and made faces at me when I told him what to do.

If I told him not to shut the door, he would wait until I walked away and then shut the door. If I told him he needed to listen and obey, he would stick his tongue out and make ridiculous faces at me. I would tell him not to bolt the gate, but he would do it as soon as I left. If Victor came to paint my toes, Paul would talk to him in Luganda, and it was clear that Paul was talking about me, making fun of the food I ate or what I did.

He began to complain about everything, mostly the food. As a child coming from the village, it was unusual to hear him complain so much. Also, I was told it was very unusual for a Ugandan child to complain so much. In their culture, a child would get in huge trouble for complaining about what food he was served, or to badmouth his elders. His behavior was surprising even to Ugandans.

It was as if I now had a teenager. That was how I knew he was not five years old, as I had been told. He was either eight or nine years old. I think he told my friend he was eight, and when asked why he told us he was five, he said that his aunt had told him to say that. This was pretty normal for adopting, so I didn't think too much of it.

A week after Sasha had been sent back, I left Paul with a sitter. Every Sunday since about the second week I had the kids, I left them with Teddy, my friend's high-school-aged daughter. She came on Sunday afternoons, and I went out with friends, either to the beach at Lake Victoria, or to hang out by the pool at Le Grand Hotel and listen to music, eat dinner and have a beer. Needless to say, I greatly looked forward to Sundays.

The kids loved Teddy, and Paul was excited that she was coming. He referred to her as his friend. That Sunday, after I got home, my friends drove Teddy home, and then called me. They had been curious and asked Teddy how she felt about my sending Sasha back, and if she would have sent Sasha or Paul back. Teddy was surprised by the question, but answered that she would have kept Sasha. Even though Sasha cried a lot, Teddy said Paul was a liar, and she had caught him hurting Sasha to make her cry. They asked why Teddy had never said anything to me about it. She replied that she didn't say anything because Paul always acted so sweet and innocent around me, how would I ever believe it?

I remember sitting on the edge of my bed, listening to this on the phone, and wanting to throw up. I already felt so much guilt about sending Sasha back. Now I had pure panic, thinking I had made such a monumental mistake. I had sent the wrong child back. I remembered I had found Sasha crying once, holding her arm and pointing at Paul, and he looked all wide-eyed with innocence and shrugged his shoulders. I assumed that Sasha was making it up, because she cried so much, and Paul was always so good, at least while Sasha was still there.

The next morning, I told Doreen what Teddy had said. Doreen then told me that she hadn't wanted to say anything, but she was concerned, because she had caught Paul lying on a number of occasions. But the most concerning thing was that, one afternoon while I was out, Paul told Doreen that I had lots of money and, if she needed any, she could just lie to me and get it.

That was shocking and disturbing. Here I had a child who was lying, not who I thought he was, older than I thought, telling people to steal from me, making fun of me in another language in front of me. It was all so unsettling. I remember feeling sick about the whole affair. I was feeling guilty concerning Sasha, and I felt fear and despair concerning Paul.

I knew that I could not send Paul back. I couldn't fail at caring for both children; I already carried the weight of sending Sasha back. It was too much. So I prayed that the ruling would be "no," but I knew that judges always ruled "yes." I kept telling myself that Paul could change. He was a child; he could change. But I was afraid.

I got through that week and the next, but I was in constant fear and stress regarding the ruling. I think I finally told my husband what I'd found out. This was the last straw for him. He was now done.

He said that after coming the first time to Uganda, he felt like, okay, maybe this would be a good thing. But after the second trip failed, he really wanted out, and only stayed in because I sounded so hopeful regarding Paul and Sasha. Now, learning that Paul may have been the instigator of Sasha's behavior, and that he was lying to me, my husband wanted out, and wanted me to quit and come home.

But I knew we were getting close to August 15. The family courts close from July 15 through August 15, and this was my lawyer's excuse as to why the ruling was taking so long. I convinced him to wait for the judge's ruling. I couldn't face my lawyer and the social worker and my friends after quitting on another child. I just hoped the judge would make that decision for us.

But on Monday morning, August 15, after nine weeks of waiting, I received an e-mail in the early morning from my lawyer. He had gotten the ruling, which was favorable for Legal Guardianship, for both children. I remember really feeling panic and despair. I messaged my husband. I was so exhausted at this point, I knew I could no longer make a decision. I told him he would have to decide – either way. I told him Paul was just a child; he could change. I also suggested that we could turn Paul back over to the foster program and take Sasha, now that we had this new insight into her behavior. But I left the decision up to him, as I no longer had any confidence in my own decision-making or judgment.

My husband had not changed his mind about adoption and sent an e-mail to the lawyer saying that he wanted to withdraw from seeking Legal Guardianship. I quickly received a phone call from my lawyer, who was considerably upset, and wanted to see me right away. I made an appointment for the next day. Thankfully, my landlady – and by now close friend – Doreen suggested that she go in with me to see my lawyer. She felt I shouldn't be alone when my lawyer confronted me.

We took two bodas to his office in Ntinde. His office was on the second floor of a shopping mall. We only had to wait about five minutes before we were ushered into his office. I'm sure he was surprised that I brought someone with me, but I was often bringing someone along with me when I dealt with him, such as Isma, the policeman, or my friend Abdul, so he just accepted Doreen's presence.

My lawyer definitely expressed his surprise and frustration about receiving my husband's e-mail, and he made it clear that he had done everything he could to get the ruling as soon as possible. My lawyer couldn't understand how my husband could withdraw now after all this time, and the same day as getting a favorable ruling on both children. I didn't say much, and I didn't explain anything about Paul's behavior. I just made it clear that my husband had made a decision, and that was it.

I asked how to go about withdrawing Legal Guardianship. Now he says it is a very difficult process. I would have to go back to court in order to withdraw the guardianship, and it could be months before getting a court date. He said I needed to go back and draft a letter stating why I was withdrawing guardianship. That was all he had to say about withdrawing.

But before I left, he said he was very surprised that I could not do this. He said he was shocked when I sent Sasha back, that I should have been able to handle a three-year-old's tantrums. He said African women had no problem handling children. By the time he was done chastising me, I was crying. I remember being in tears, saying to him that I knew I was a failure.

He turned to Doreen and asked her if she had children, and Doreen said that she had a fourteen-year-old daughter. "So you know," he said, "she should have been able to handle Sasha. How did you raise your daughter?" Doreen just calmly said, "When she was bad, I caned her and, you know, Christine couldn't do that."

"Oh, yes, you're right." That was Thomas's only response. I was so thankful for Doreen. After that we left and, in the parking lot, Doreen was so angry. She knew that Thomas was trying to get her to agree with him. Her response was that he was greatly to blame for this whole situation anyway, taking so long to get a court date, and then nine weeks for the ruling, adding all this time and stress.

I returned to the house and messaged Ruth, the social worker, what was going on and that I didn't want to send Paul back to the village. Her response in messaging me was, "It's a disappointment and annoying. It's too much." She said she needed to come to my place and talk that week. I told her I was trying to get Paul into a boarding school. She arranged to come at 10 a.m. on Friday, as I told her I had an appointment at around 2:30 p.m.

In the meantime, I found out that Doreen and Esther's mother worked for Watoto church, a very large church in Kampala, famous for the African Children's Choir. The church had a boarding school for orphans. This was ideal, because most boarding schools sent the kids home to family over the breaks in between the three terms. But Watoto's program kept the kids year-round and sent them to camps over the breaks.

They also gave the kids a place to stay all the way through college. The best part was that, if the child was not good academically, they had a trade skills program to give them the best possibility of a future. I immediately called the contact that Doreen gave me and talked to a woman named Sarah, who worked with admitting children into the program. I explained how I had guardianship, but could no longer pursue the adoption and wanted to sponsor Paul in this program. She sent me the application via e-mail and asked me to return the supporting documents to her.

Because the adoption process is so thorough, I already had all the necessary documents. The Watoto program required letters from probation officers stating that the child was an orphan or, that if he had relatives, he was still in such need that he would qualify for such a program. As stated:

Babies/children who qualify for WCCM care and protection

- *Orphans. Children/babies who have lost both their parents and whose relatives are unable or not willing to adopt the child and provide a fundamentally safe and social environment for the child.*
- *Abandoned/abused/neglected/destitute babies/children. Cases must be well documented by the Police, hospitals, local authorities, Probation and Social Welfare Office or children's temporary institutions/referral sources.*

- *Babies/children whose parents are serving long-term prison sentences. Available family is not willing or able to take on care and protection of baby/child.*
- *Documents should be obtained in conjunction with prison authorities. Any other worthy cause. This category of children/babies is subject to thorough investigations being made to verify the evidence that the proposed child falls within the above categories. (a detailed report justifying admission written and submitted).*

I had death certificates for both of Paul's parents, letters from the probation officers and from the local village Chairman stating that Paul was an orphan and that living relatives were not financially able to care for him. I had signatures from his aunts and uncles stating they gave up any guardianship rights. It was easy to fill out the application, and I felt hopeful that I would hear back from her soon.

I had to include the phone number of his Aunt Kate, with whom he had most recently been living. Sarah messaged me to say that after she looked at the paperwork and called his aunt, she would contact me to set up a time for an interview. I was already thinking about how I could visit him once a year and send him letters and packages. I felt like this was such a good opportunity for Paul.

He had never attached himself to me; in fact, he had never seemed that interested in America or going there. In more than ten weeks with me, he had refused to learn any English, and he made fun of my customs, food and habits. I felt like this boarding school program could really change his life, and I would do my best to be a good friend and sponsor, even if I couldn't be his mother.

I messaged Ruth and told her that I had applied for this program. She messaged back saying she thought he should come home for holidays and after University. She said she would talk this over with Pastor Luke and see the way forward. I remember thinking it was odd she was so concerned he wouldn't come home for holidays, when I was about to adopt him and take him to America where they might never see him again! This program seemed the perfect answer if I couldn't adopt him.

By Thursday I had returned all the applications and supporting documents to Sarah. By Friday morning at 10 a.m. I was waiting for Ruth to arrive. Doreen, Esther and Doreen's daughter, Anne, were in the house with me, watching movies and cooking, while I was sewing. Paul was around the back of the house hanging out with Fred the guard.

Ruth was always late, but this day she was particularly late – without any call or explanation. She finally showed up sometime after noon. When she entered the house, it was clear that she was annoyed with me. She sat in the chair next to me, talked with Doreen and Esther a little in Luganda about her new hair style, then she sent messages on her phone and ignored me for over two hours.

Esther and I made lunch, offered her some, and she still ignored me. We were all struck by how angry she must be, and I was beginning to be annoyed. After eating, and while Doreen and I were in the kitchen washing dishes, Ruth got up, went out around to the back of the house and started talking in Luganda to Paul. Doreen was extremely upset because, in their culture, it was so rude to be invited to someone's house, ignore the host, then, without explanation, leave the house to go and have a private conversation with a child.

Doreen sent Esther to tell Paul he was needed in the house. Paul immediately came, but Ruth did not. Instead, she stayed and talked with Fred, loudly complaining in English about me. Everyone in the house could hear her, and now the insult was clear.

After a bit, Ruth came back around the front of the house, but she received a phone call and stayed outside talking for a very long time. After another hour or more had passed, she came back into the house and said she needed to talk to me. By this time, I was extremely annoyed. I waited for Ruth to continue and she informed me that she had just spoken with a woman from Watoto and she was annoyed with her. Ruth claimed that Watoto seemed like they would not take Paul because he had family. She said the woman didn't want to listen and really didn't seem agreeable to taking Paul.

I was confused, because their application clearly stated that if there are living family members, there just needed to be a reason why the child should be submitted to the program. They needed necessary documents to prove this, and I had all the documents, signatures and more.

Shortly after telling me this, Ruth left, apparently with nothing else she wanted to talk about.

That Sunday night, I had a sitter for Paul, and I was with friends relaxing. I began to get messages from Ruth, which I showed to my Ugandan friends. They immediately told me to trust them, and only respond when and with what they told me to write. They were also suspicious, especially after Ruth's recent behavior, and yet she started messaging me with "Hope we will be friends forever."

But after a few minutes, she messaged, "Roger told us you are supposed to make a donation of $1,000 to the foster program coz the cases was done, are you aware about it or not?" My friends advised me to simply reply that, when I get back to America, I will work on it with my husband, because right now I didn't have the money. That response seemed to make her happy, at least for a few days.

Monday morning I received an e-mail from Sarah stating that Watoto would not be able to accept Paul into its program. She wrote that she and Ruth had spoken on the phone and decided that Paul would be better off with his family in the village. She said that Ruth would help him be reunited with his family. I was greatly surprised, as I knew they took in children who had living relatives, and I knew Paul met the qualifications, since he met the more stringent qualifications of being given Legal Guardianship and adopted out of the country.

It was clear that her decision was based on her conversation with Ruth. I was very angry and could only assume this was about money. Somehow she thought having him back in the foster program would gain more, perhaps by finding another family to adopt him, and getting another $1,000 donation.

I was trying to do the best for Paul and, for whatever reason, Ruth had sabotaged a great opportunity for him. I was furious. After speaking with Doreen and Esther, we all agreed there wasn't much I could do except turn Paul back over to Ruth and the care of the foster program.

I messaged Ruth what Sarah had e-mailed and that, after speaking with her (Ruth), she had agreed that Paul should be relocated back with family in the village.

I told Ruth that she needed to come and get Paul as soon as possible, as the longer he remained with me, the more difficult it would be. Ruth wrote back – this time very annoyed. She claimed that she tried to convince Sarah to accept Paul into the program, but that Sarah refused and wanted to resettle him with his relatives. Ruth went on to say *she* was disappointed a long time ago, and what could be done now with Paul, because a lot of time had been wasted.

I responded by saying, "I think the best course of action, according to what everyone has discussed, is to get him back to his relatives as soon as possible, and perhaps you will find him another family. I would like you to come get him Wednesday if possible."

It took her a couple days to respond, and she said she would come pick him up on Thursday. I asked her to come in the morning.

On Wednesday, August 26, I received the following message from Ruth:

> *Am sorry to ask you please will you pay the donation or not because Paul is also back to the home as per now. The foster program in Kassanda has no funding, Paul has to go back to the school, there are no school fees. Will you be able to support him with school fees and other scholastic materials? I thought he will now receive a better education but am now just disappointed. When I take these kids back I look stupid and ashamed in front of Kate, and I myself feel guilty and sorry. The kids had expectations but its like you are violating their rights. They've lost hope in their life according to the experience they have faced. It affects them after you are showing them a different life and then you disappoint them.*

Even now, writing this two months after learning the whole truth, I still feel ashamed. I was angry at Ruth for ruining Paul's chance of getting into Watoto, but I knew what she was saying to me was true, and the guilt was a weight so heavy. I despised myself for being such a failure. I knew that if I'd been better able to parent Sasha and Paul, if I were stronger, braver, more loving, then I could have been a good mother and enjoyed being with them.

I wasn't used to quitting or failing or not being strong enough. But this whole experience was filled with fear and shame and misery. I knew now that I was not worthy. I did not deserve to parent any child. All I could think of was Paul back in the village in poverty and depression. I knew I was at fault. I had disappointed two children, two orphans, perhaps broken their hearts, and I was so ashamed. I despised myself. I've never felt so low or despicable in my life.

Later that day, I received a phone call from Roger, telling me he had heard that I was sending the children back. Both Ruth and Pastor Luke had been calling him, upset and wanting him to fix it. I told Roger it wasn't his fault at all, and why would they be placing responsibility on him? He said it was because he had introduced me to the program.

He said Ruth asked him to come with her on Thursday to pick up Paul. He asked me if that would be okay? I told him of course he could come, but that I had already told her I didn't have the $1,000 donation, and would work on it when I got home, and that I really needed Ruth to take Paul on Thursday because it was becoming so difficult. He said they would arrive in the morning.

The next morning, Doreen, Esther and Anne decided to stay close by, so they were in the house eating breakfast, and Paul was on the floor watching a cartoon on TV. Roger called, saying that they would arrive soon. I was in my room when they arrived; Doreen told me they were there. I heard them walk into the house, so I came out to the sitting area, where I was surprised to see Ruth, Roger and a third lady.

Ruth was obviously angry, and her mannerisms were aggressive. I found out later that Ruth led them right into the house without knocking, and then asked Esther what she was laughing at! Esther calmly replied that it was customary to smile and greet guests when they are invited into a house.

I asked the three of them if we could talk outside, since Paul was sitting right there, and they followed me out to the front of the compound. We sat on the cement wall in front of the adjacent rental house. I was confused, and I remember feeling such a burden and almost fear. Mostly, I remember knowing that I was guilty and would just have to take the criticisms and comments and the shame.

Roger introduced the third person as his friend, Laura, who came just to help talk through the situation. I got the impression that she came as a mediator. I remember being so confused as to why she was there, and I was trying to figure out what their agenda was, but I was also confused because Laura seemed familiar.

Laura started out by talking and continued to control the conversation the entire hour they were there. She said she knew a little of what was going on, but could I explain, especially, how I had met Roger and been given a referral with these kids. I began to explain how my last referral had fallen apart and, before I could continue, Laura interrupted me. "Did you work with an American agency?" My brain seemed so slow in catching up with recognizing her. I admitted that we had used an American agency with the first referral. She said yes, she thought she recognized me. "I worked with you and your husband with James and Kira."

I was completely shocked. What were the odds that she was now sitting here. I remembered thinking that Laura had not only condoned us reuniting James and Kira with their mom, but she had thanked me at the time, over a year ago. Now I was embarrassed to be sitting here, explaining that our second attempt ended with trafficked children, and now I had sent the third set of children back.

I was so ashamed and knew she must think I am a total American flake. I must have seemed like a crazy person. I briefly explained that things were proving difficult with Sasha and now Paul. I explained that I had tried to get Paul into Watoto's program, but that the director and Ruth had decided he needed to be back with family in the village, so I needed Ruth to take him back that day.

Ruth said they could not take him that day because I had Legal Guardianship, and they needed a legal document from my lawyer stating that I revoked guardianship. I agreed to get the letter that afternoon.

Laura said that her program might be able to find Paul a new family, and they would want me to write a letter stating why I was not accepting Legal Guardianship. She said I needed to state the reason. "Is it because your husband made a decision or because something is wrong with the children? Because if something is wrong…we need to know."

I knew that was an odd question but, again, I was confused by all of this, and Laura was so aggressive, I couldn't figure out what her motivation was behind these questions. Ruth jumped in at that point with the question about the "fee" of $1,000 dollars. Laura said yes, hadn't I made that agreement? I said that Roger had mentioned it last fall when I had begun the process with this foster program, but that I didn't have a written agreement because that would amount to buying children, and that was illegal.

Laura immediately turned to Ruth, and said, "Yes, she is right; it can't be a fee, but could only be a donation." But, Laura said, I could still have my lawyer draft a document saying I would donate $1,000 to them, and have it legally notarized. At this point, Laura became very aggressive and said to me, "You need to own up to what you did. This is between you and your conscience." She went on to say that now I had disappointed six children.

She said I needed to be held accountable for what I'd done. She said I needed to go to the village myself and apologize to Paul's relatives and the pastor and the villagers for returning Paul and Sasha. She turned to Roger and told him he was also guilty for not looking into the kind of person I was when he allowed me to get a referral for these kids.

She told Roger he needed to drive me and Paul to the village. She kept reiterating that I had disappointed these children and ruined their future; I needed to be accountable. At first I told her I didn't feel comfortable doing this. I would rather send Paul back with Ruth, but Laura was adamant and aggressive, insisting I needed to own up to this and be accountable.

She also said that "they wouldn't beat me." So I just agreed to go, not knowing what else to do. At this point, I remember crying and getting choked up, but telling her that she couldn't possibly make me feel more guilty than I already did. I told her I knew I was a failure.

The meeting concluded with my having agreed to get a letter from my lawyer stating that I revoked guardianship. I also agreed to go the next day with Roger to take Paul back to the village and apologize.

As soon as they left, I was flooded with so much emotion. I went into my room and cried for a short amount of time, then came back out to explain to Doreen and Esther what had happened. They were both so angry about what had occurred, telling me that it was crazy for three social workers to show up.

At this point, I called my lawyer to ask about coming in to his office for the letter. He told me that revoking guardianship is not an easy process, that now I had to go back to court before the judge.

He said it could be months before we could get a court date, and he didn't know how the judge would even respond. My lawyer was obviously annoyed and made it seem that this process would be almost impossible. He told me to come in the next morning to discuss it.

As soon as I got off the phone, I was informed that Victor had arrived. He was the young man who came to paint my toenails – a good time to sit and be distracted and relieve some stress. Doreen had to go to town, but Esther and I sat outside while Victor began to scrub my feet in a bucket of water.

That is when Esther told me what had been happening while I was with the three social workers.

Doreen and Esther had been suspicious, since Doreen had a degree related to social work, and Esther was currently pursuing a degree in that field. They felt it was completely unprofessional and odd for Ruth to show up with two other social workers. When they saw how aggressively Ruth was behaving and how the three of them were talking to me at length, they began to wonder if something else could be happening.

Esther asked Paul if he understood what was happening. He calmly said he was going back to the village. Esther asked how he knew that, and he said because he saw "mommy" packing his suitcases. They asked if he would like going back to live with his aunt. He said he would be living with his mom.

At first Esther thought, okay, he must call his aunt his mom, but she questioned him again, saying, "You mean your aunt, not your real mom."

"No," Paul said, he lived with his real mom. Esther said, "But you lived with your aunt, and Sasha also lived with you, right?"

At this point, Paul began to get confused and he even said, "Oh, that's not what I was supposed to say." Now it was clear to Esther that someone was lying.

So they began to ask more questions, and as she was telling me this while I'm getting my nails painted, I remember feeling nauseous, and felt a horrible sinking feeling in my stomach. At first I was in complete disbelief. This could not be happening – could not be true. This had happened to me once before. Paul was just misunderstanding.

But she called Paul over, and we began asking more questions. When Doreen came back from town, and we all began to ask questions, and the truth came spilling out. Paul had been holding in these lies for ten weeks. He had been coached by Ruth, by Pastor Luke, by Kate, by his mother, Patricia, and by his grandfather. He was supposed to tell me that he was five years old, and that both his parents were dead. He was supposed to tell me he lived with his Aunt Kate and with Sasha.

In reality, he lived with his mother in a house next door! In fact, the three times I had visited his mother (whom I believed was an aunt in a distant village), she hid from sight, and Paul pretended to come out of Kate's house. I even have a picture of him and Kate and Sasha sitting in the corner of the small one-room house with one mattress on the cold cement floor.

Paul now told us that his father was alive and well, living on the other side of the village; in fact, he had seen him just before coming to court. Paul's parents did not get along, and often Paul and his mother would sneak to his father's house and steal jackfruit off the trees. Then his father would come to his mother's house and verbally abuse them. Paul thought this was funny as he laughingly told us this story.

Esther asked him whose funeral he had gone to, and Paul said he'd never been to a burial. She asked whose grave was in the pictures I had. In Ugandan culture, family members are usually buried on family property behind the house. Paul told us that nobody was buried behind either of his parents' houses or any relatives' houses that he knew of. When we looked up the name in my court documents, Paul confirmed that his father is Edward, but he is not dead.

The woman whose death certificate I had, who was supposed to be Paul's mother, was unknown to him. Her name is Kotida Nakatte. Paul said he had no relatives named Kotida Nakatte; in fact, the only one he knew with that name was the woman living with the pastor.

Paul also told us that Kate had "found" Sasha outside the church and had taken her home. He said Sasha's mother came back for her, but Kate and Ruth told her that she couldn't have Sasha back, as she had already been promised to a white lady. When I heard this, I was filled with fury. It was all too familiar – the stealing and selling of these children.

I was still in shock that this was happening again but, as the truth was pouring out of Paul, there were too many details and facts to be false. During our questioning, Paul got worried and said, "They will be mad at me for ruining everything." I was angry that they had put such pressure on a child to lie in order that they could gain.

After getting all of the facts we could from Paul, I rewarded him for telling the truth with a pair of binoculars and an orange Fanta. Then I took a boda over to the guest house to talk with Connie and Jack to get their advice. Understandably, they were shocked that this could have happened to me again. They advised me to get help from Abdul once again and, after placing a call, I arranged to meet him the next morning at Freedom City (a shopping mall), where he would pick me up and I would spend the morning at the chicken farm with him. Also, I texted my lawyer and Roger, making excuses to both of them and putting off meeting them until another week. I didn't want either, especially Roger, to know what I had discovered.

The next morning in the van on the way to the farm, I explained as best I could to my friend Abdul what was going on. As usual, he quietly took in the situation, then made a firm and determined plan. It was Friday and he wanted me to take a boda back to my house, get all the documents on Paul I could find, with names of relatives and death certificates, then label them where it was helpful, and send them with a boda driver back to him. He would take the documents with him to Kassanda and find out the truth.

In the midst of all the emotions I was experiencing, I still recognized the blessing in knowing Abdul, who was such a good friend to me, and also for being at his chicken farm near Lake Victoria, where I had spent so much time.

I wrote this journal entry while sitting next to the lake, waiting on Abdul.

August 28

> *At Lake Victoria, Scripture Union (camp). Came with Abdul to talk about this new issue with Paul. He's going to investigate for me tomorrow. So peaceful here listening to the waves. Cool breeze. Sun warm on my neck.*
>
> *I love Africa.*

Around 5 a.m. the next morning, Abdul called a policeman whom I had hired to investigate the referral last fall, and asked him to go to Kassanda with him to look into the facts. The policeman was understandably rattled and confused, because he knew Abdul was going to determine if he (the policeman) had been tricked and deceived with his investigation, or if he'd been bought off.

Abdul and the policeman spent the day in Kassanda and Mubende, finding out the truth and confronting people. On Sunday, I met Abdul again at Freedom City, this time to spend the day on the farm, helping vaccinate 4,000 baby chicks, as well as receiving Abdul's report. Thankfully, the policeman was innocent and, as we were to find out, this whole affair had been well planned and facts were falsified.

The entire weekend, Doreen and Esther were watching Paul at the house for me. Again, I am so thankful for their care and friendship. They were able to help me stay calm and focused in finding out the truth.

Sunday morning I met Abdul again at Freedom City. We sat at a restaurant for a bit while I ordered some snacks for all of the workers at the chicken farm to enjoy after we completed the vaccinations. Abdul began to tell me what he and the policeman had discovered. First, they went to the foster program office and found nobody there, so they proceeded to the address of Patricia, who Paul now confessed was his mother.

Abdul was first shocked to find out that Patricia lived next door to Kate. Their houses were a few feet apart, whereas I had been told that Patricia lived in a village some hours away. They found Patricia at home, hanging laundry. Abdul said it didn't take much at all for her to admit the truth. She broke down fairly quickly and admitted that she was Paul's mother. Abdul said she was very obviously scared at having been caught.

She claimed that Ruth and Kate had forced her to lie. She also claimed she only thought Paul was going to get educated in Kampala, not be adopted in America. This we all knew was not true; even in court, the judge asked her and each witness if they understood "adoption" and that Paul and Sasha would be leaving for America to live with a new family, and that all relatives would be giving up their rights to these kids.

I believe that Abdul was stern, but not unkind, in his questioning. He told her that as long as she admitted the truth and helped sort this out, then he would do his best to keep her from facing something worse, such as prison. Next, they went to another nearby house where they found Pastor Luke. He also quickly broke down and admitted the truth. Both the pastor and mother agreed to meet in a restaurant in Freedom City the next morning so that I could meet and discuss the truth and what would happen next.

Abdul also went to meet/confront Kate, who was caring again for Sasha. Kate was very aggressive and at first denied the truth completely. Abdul told me she angered him so much that he almost had her arrested. She kept angrily complaining and yelling about me, saying that I had sent Sasha back without any money. This, of course, was not true. I sent Sasha and Ruth back to the village with a suitcase full of toys and clothes and a sum of money. Now, whether Ruth kept all the money or

Kate was lying, I will never know. Finally, after a threat of arrest, Kate admitted the truth, but she blamed most of it on Ruth.

The rest of Abdul's investigation uncovered quite a bit. Documents had been falsified and the photos of the gravesites were fake. He tried to talk with the Local Chairman, but his sons said he was visiting his "goldmine," which gave Abdul and me a good laugh. I'd never heard about gold in Uganda, but I suppose there could be hope in anything.

I spent that day on the chicken farm, focusing on vaccinating baby chicks. This involved a handful of Ugandan workers and putting eyedrops in the eyes of 4,000 chicks. You can't be stressed and angry when you have to concentrate on getting the vaccine in the eye of a chick without poking its eye out! It was also a challenge to get them to keep their eyes open, as some chicks would actually pass out or play dead, which frankly always made me laugh. But holding little yellow fuzzballs all day and focusing on the task was a blessing. There was also a new kitten they were introducing to the farm to help with the rat population. Kittens and chicks are excellent therapy!

On the drive home, I had time to get angry again. Abdul called Ruth and arranged to meet her in a few minutes at a restaurant. Abdul had an issue with a tire, so he dropped the van, me, and two other workers off at a mechanic's shop, and he took a boda to meet Ruth. He was gone at least an hour. When he came back, he told me that he arrived at the restaurant and couldn't find Ruth. He saw a few young women sitting, and since he didn't know who Ruth was, he called to see who would pick up the phone. Ruth answered the phone, but he didn't see any young women on a phone in the restaurant.

As it turns out, Ruth was hiding in the bathroom and peering out to see if Abdul had arrived with any police. I think at this point she was beginning to test his patience. She came out eventually and, although she denied everything at first, finally she admitted to being in on the entire deception. Abdul had her agree to meet us at Freedom City the next morning with Patricia and Pastor Luke.

Unknown to them, Abdul was also having Isma, the police detective who helped me with the last trafficking case, come as well – this time in uniform.

The next morning, I arrived early at the restaurant in Freedom City, sat in a booth, ordered a mocha, and began to take notes. I was nervous and stressed, but this time I was filled with so much anger. It was close to fury. (I have one personality trait that my sister, Miriam, has always pointed out. When I am most angry, I become calm and clearheaded.)

That morning, I was angry – angrier than I had ever been in my life. Some of it was righteous anger, and some was selfish anger for being in this position again. I took my notebook and wrote out numbered bullet points of everything I wanted Ruth, Patricia and Pastor Luke to answer for. I wrote out what I wanted to say to them. I didn't want to forget or be persuaded otherwise.

The last time I'd been in this position with Benjamin and Anna, I had been so scared and nervous and stressed. That confrontation with my lawyers was handled by Abdul and Isma. I was silent during most of that interview. This time, when Abdul arrived, I asked him to let me conduct the interview. I wanted to be the one doing the talking. I asked him to jump in whenever he wanted or needed to, but I would like to lead. He agreed right away, saying he would open up the discussion, then hand it over to me.

I had been in this restaurant before with Abdul and Jack. It served a lunch buffet of local food, the coffee was decent, and the service is good. But it is dark, with red carpeting and dark tables and chairs, booths lining one side. It is a place I will always remember but, because of the circumstances, never enjoy. The place suited the purpose, though, and it seemed to be an appropriate venue to confront the lies and draw them out of the shadows.

When Pastor Luke, Patricia and Ruth all arrived together, Abdul and I moved to a table large enough to accommodate all of us. On one side were Patricia and Pastor Luke. Across from Pastor Luke, I was sitting next to Abdul, and on his far side, Ruth. About fifteen minutes into the confrontation, Isma showed up in uniform and sat next to Pastor Luke. When Isma showed up, you could see fear as Pastor Luke, Patricia and Ruth fell silent staring at him.

To open the meeting, Abdul said that, although we were not meeting under good circumstances, he felt we should open with a prayer. He asked the pastor to please pray over the meeting. Pastor Luke complied but, ironically, his prayer made me even angrier. He prayed that the truth would be told! These were the same words that the International Director from my American agency had said when he had prayed that I would tell the truth.

Today's prayer was a sign that I was about to be confronted by an undercurrent of evil and lies. I know that it was not a coincidence that those same words were spoken, just as the same lies were about to be told – lies that destroy families and exploit children. I don't know whether the type of people who deal with trafficking children convince themselves they are championing the truth, or if, what I think is more likely, they use lies and distort the truth and attempt to lie and bully their way into exploiting children.

It felt like the conversation that day was at least two hours long but, in reality, I think it lasted maybe an hour. I began by telling Pastor Luke, Patricia and Ruth that there had better be no repercussions for Paul, as he was just a child, and they had used him and taught him to lie. He was innocent, and now he was scared. They had taught him to lie to a muzungu in order to get "stuff." He never saw me as a mother, but as a cash machine, because that is what they taught him. He was an innocent child; they were accountable. I warned them that I had better not find out that they punished Paul for telling the truth, or else....

Even then I knew it was an empty threat. They were scared, and I didn't know what else to say to protect Paul. I pray that he was not held accountable for "ruining their plan." As Abdul later said, "For a child to have the courage to tell the truth under such circumstances is remarkable."

I think the first question I confronted them with (looking directly at Ruth) was, where did they get the money to pay for all the false documents? Did they use my money to buy the death certificates? Did they use the money I paid to facilitate paperwork to buy off the Probation Officer and the Local Council and the witnesses? Had they included me in this child trafficking by using my money?

I didn't give them the chance to be innocent. I just questioned them under the assumption of guilt. Yet they still denied they were involved.

Patricia didn't speak English, so questions were answered by Ruth and Pastor Luke, saying they were innocent and didn't know any of this at first. Ruth blamed Roger, then they both blamed Kate. I was furious. I told them they were wasting my time. If they were going to deny everything and lie, there was no point for me to speak with them.

Abdul then stepped in and said the same thing: that we knew the truth already and they had admitted their wrongdoing. If they were going to lie now, we could stop wasting our time, and Isma could just escort them to the police station. Now we saw real fear as they were practically crying, asking us to continue, that they would answer, and, yes, they were guilty.

Then I asked if Paul's father knew any of this – that he was being adopted and sent to America? Abdul translated to Patricia and, as we already knew, she said "no," the father had no idea.

At one point, Abdul asked if this organization was set up to make money. At first, they denied it, and Pastor Luke said "no," while Ruth made various excuses. They claimed their organization was ethical to help children, but adopting Paul and Sasha was all Kate's idea.

Abdul pointed out that they had asked for money for paperwork from me and for documents to adopt Paul and Sasha. Wasn't it, therefore, a business to make money, especially as they were taking advantage of me and falsifying all the documents? Ruth put all the blame on Roger, saying he had told Ruth to demand the $1,000.

At this point, Abdul began to lose his temper, telling them that it was easy to blame two people who weren't there. Yet Pastor Luke and Ruth were the two people who started the foster program; they were co-CEOs of the organization. Therefore, if they were making money from adopting out children, they were a business. Abdul told them their business needed to be shut down. They began to panic.

I continued my questioning, asking them about Sasha. Was she really abandoned? At first they said "yes," and I again accused them of lying, because I had the truth from Paul. So Pastor Luke admitted that Sasha was not really abandoned, they knew who her parents were, and both lived in the village. I was so angry and asked how they had the right to take Sasha, especially when her mother had come for her and they had refused to give Sasha to her. Pastor Luke made an excuse, saying Sasha's parents had no home really, and the mother was "kind of a prostitute." I told him it was not his place to moralize if she was a fit mother or not. According to American and Ugandan laws, you cannot take someone's child without permission. It was completely illegal and immoral to sell Sasha.

At this point, Pastor Luke folded his hands together and began begging me for mercy, saying this was a mistake. It was the first time they had done this, and they were just trying to help all the kids. It was a mistake.

For a few minutes, I sat there quietly. Abdul was saying something. I remember my heart softening a little, feeling sorry for Pastor Luke since he seemed scared and sincere. But then there was a voice in the back of my head reminding me that evil can come in the form of soft words and penitent faces. I snapped out of it; I knew they were all lies. So I told them something I had learned from my uncle. "A good tree cannot bear bad fruit."

Pastor Luke and Ruth claimed that their organization is truly good; they just made one mistake. But what they did was so wrong and so evil. It was the fruit of their organization and, therefore, I did not believe the rest of the organization was good. How was I to believe it was just one mistake and not a business set up to profit from selling children?

I told them I had heard their apologies, but I was not there to police their organization, and I could not investigate the case of every child they have up for adoption. I asked why they did not use their donated funds to help sustain these families, instead of profiting by selling them overseas. I said to Pastor Luke, "You are a pastor and, Ruth, you are a social worker. It was your jobs to fight for these kids. Paul and Sasha matter. They were not disposable for a cause. You were supposed to look out for them and, instead, you used them for your own gain."

They claimed this was all a mistake, but they used two children for the supposed good of the rest. If they cared about kids, how could they use these two? I told them, "Shame on you." His whole family used Paul and manipulated him to gain money. How would he ever trust family or the church again? By this time, I was white hot with anger.

I turned to Ruth and told her I was mostly angry with her – first, because of the overwhelming guilt and shame she made me feel for not being able to be a mother to Sasha and to Paul. How was I ever to be a mother to a little girl who was stolen from her parents and who was so confused she thought everyone was supposed to be her mother now? How was I supposed to ever be a mother to Paul, who knew he was being sold by his family purely for financial gain?

He would only ever see me as a cash machine. He would never love or respect me as a parent because he knew who his parents were, and he had been taught to lie and manipulate the white woman to get things. Ruth's accusation of disappointing Sasha and Paul and ruining their lives was inexcusable, especially since she, Ruth, had ruined Paul's chances of getting into Watoto's program simply because they would have done an investigation on his family and found out the truth. She had used these children and placed guilt and shame on my head, when all along she was to blame.

At this point, Ruth was almost crying and said in a quiet voice that she was sorry. I remember that I was shaking when I said all those things to Pastor Luke and Ruth. I was so angry, and the full weight of their guilt was staring at me around that table.

The meeting had to end at that point, because Abdul had set up another meeting in Kampala with Roger and Laura. It had really bothered him that they had shown up at my house, and he wanted to know how involved they were. So we ended this meeting with Abdul heading out and Isma remaining to try to take Patricia's statement.

But Patricia was so scared that she was getting flustered and mixed up, not able to remember simple facts. Isma decided she needed to come to the station that afternoon after she calmed down. He did get her to say that Kate and Ruth had approached her with the plan, and it was their idea to fake the death certificate of Paul's father.

Abdul asked me to wait at Freedom City until he was finished talking with Laura and Roger. I ended up waiting all day. The interview took him some time, as they kept lying at the beginning. He finally got the truth out of them and then came back to pick me up and tell me their involvement. All this time, I had been hoping that Roger was innocent. He had been introduced to me by my friend Mary, and he had seemed so sincere. I had even gone to his college graduation party. Surely he was trustworthy and innocent in all this. That was my hope. I was completely wrong.

Roger claims that at first he didn't know that Paul and Sasha had families, but at some point in the process he discovered the truth and chose to go along with the lie. At first he was in close contact with Ruth, doing paperwork for the two children but, at some point, he claims that Ruth stopped contacting him. He says he didn't have any contact or involvement until right before court. Again, he didn't hear from Ruth after court until I tried to send Paul back.

Then Ruth panicked and called him. He had a conversation with his "boss," and they discussed my past attempts at adopting. On his boss's advice, he looked up my caseworker with my American agency, Laura, and contacted her. He and his boss decided to bring Laura in on it, in order for her to shame me and guilt me into giving the $1,000. Then the three caseworkers would split the money.

I was sitting at Freedom City with Abdul in the open area at the mall. I was so angry that I couldn't speak. I was emotional and in tears. I think this is when my naiveté and trust snapped like a cord stretched too tightly. I was such a fool, such an idiot. I thought of all the time and money and affection and anticipation, all the guilt and shame and heartache. I couldn't take any of that back; I couldn't change any of that. I was consumed with anger.

Even now, as I write this two months later, I feel the same pain and anger. It's an emptiness, where I thought something was good and discovered that it didn't exist. I've always been an optimist – always wanted to forgive and think the best of people. I've always wanted to solve conflict and be at peace with everyone. I lost all that.

I know I'm a different person now. I don't want to be dramatic or self-indulgent, but I know I've changed. I no longer trust, and I see how much of a fool I was.

In Uganda, if a crime is committed and you want a result, you are the "complainant" and have to pay the costs. I paid Isma the fees for him and his investigators to travel to Kassanda, investigate and write their report under a "General Inquiry File." Once they finish their investigation, they will turn it over to the courts, which will then most certainly determine to shut down the foster program.

Pastor Luke, Ruth, Kate and all involved deserve to go to prison. But this would require me to pay for court, and I would have had to stay longer in Uganda to testify against them. They could make up any accusations against me, or even try to harm me, in order to stay out of prison. Isma and Abdul advised me against pursuing this mess in court, stating that getting the foster program in Kassanda shut down should be the priority.

After that meeting, I met with Isma a week later and he gave me the results of their investigation. They had gone on September 2, 2015, to Mubende and Kassanda. Isma couldn't reach Pastor Luke or Ruth, as they had turned their phones off. Isma and Abdul went to the office first, but it was closed. Next they found Kate at her house. He interrogated her, but she was so aggressive and uncooperative that he wanted to arrest her.

In order to arrest her in a district outside of his jurisdiction, he had to have the Local Council chairman. When Isma and Abdul drove to find him, he was at his gold mine again. They drove to the mine and picked him up, bringing him back to Kate's house. Now she told the truth and made her statement, including her involvement. Isma said that it was clear from what the Chairman said that he had warned the foster program before that they had better clean up their act. Isma got the impression that this was not the first adoption case gone bad from this organization, even though Pastor Luke and Ruth claimed I was the first victim.

Kate claimed that Paul had been giving his mom, Patricia, a hard time and, financially, she couldn't care for him, so Kate and Ruth decided he would be better off adopted. Patricia was Kate's sister, and they convinced her of their plan.

Isma felt that Kate was still lying about much of the case. He said from all their investigating, it was clear that Kate and Ruth were truly the masterminds behind all of this. Kate was the one who coached Paul on what to say and lie about. The pastor, Patricia and other relatives were in on it, but Ruth was really the one planning it all. In fact, Isma said, it appeared that Ruth hardly ever went to Kassanda or Mubende; she spent almost all her time in Mukono in Kampala.

Isma said it truly was an organization that has raised suspicions. The pastor had a hidden agenda. There were at least eight kids living with him at his house, and when anyone would visit, he brought at least 12 more kids in. He claimed they were all orphans. Isma said they were not being well cared for at all.

Isma said the chairman brought in the father, Edward, who had just discovered the truth. He had become suspicious when he heard that Pastor Luke and Patricia had gone to Kampala (when I had met them). So when Patricia got back, he confronted her and asked where his son Paul was. Patricia broke down and told the truth. He was furious; he went to get the police to have her arrested, but when they came back, she had disappeared. Isma said nobody knew where she was at this time. Paul's father was truly innocent and unsuspecting in all of this.

Isma said it seemed from his interview with Kate that she was lying about Roger, trying to hide his involvement. But we already knew Roger was guilty. Furthermore, Roger did all the initial paperwork on Paul and Sasha. Roger knew that I had hired a police officer to do a private investigation.

How was the officer given so many false statements and documents? The guilty parties had to know he was coming, and Roger is the only one who could have told them that. Isma and I now believe that Roger had to have been involved from the beginning.

That Friday, Abdul picked Paul and me up at the house, and again we went to Freedom City. This time, Paul had to give his statement to a policewoman, while I gave my statement to Isma. It was my second time giving a statement to Ugandan police. Even now I could tell you how they have to mark the paper and write the statement out. By giving my statement and stating that I relinquished Legal Guardianship, I no longer was liable for Paul or Sasha. I had a document signed by police that I was not responsible for these children since they had parents.

When we finished, I bought lunch for Paul and Isma. The plan was that Isma would take Paul home with him that night. Then in the morning, he would take Paul to Kassanda and turn him over to his father. He would also try to track down Sasha to find out where she was. He told me later that he discovered Sasha was back in the program, being cared for by the foster program. Her parents were said to be "up and down a lot," meaning they were not in the village at that time.

Paul knew he was leaving me and going back to the village. The only question he asked me was, "Will I get to go to school?" I told him I would try. I don't think he understood, but he was excited to stay overnight with a policeman. Isma dropped me off on a busy street in Kampala. I didn't even have time to hug Paul as he was in the back seat of the car. However, I turned to him and told him he'd be okay, and that it wasn't goodbye forever – that I would see him again. I hope there is truth in that.

I had one week left in Uganda after saying goodbye to Paul. I was trying to get home by September 19 for my brother's wedding. I spent that last week visiting with friends and meeting different people I had been working on projects with. Honestly, I wasn't ready to leave yet. Even with all the bad that had happened, I still loved Kampala. I have friends who deeply touched and inspired me. I met people who showed me compassion and love and support in such a difficult time. I made friends that I will have for life. To them I owe so much.

Ready to Head Home

After saying my goodbyes to all of these friends and more, the day came for me to fly home. My good friends Emmanuel, Collin, Matts and Jonah picked me up to take me to the airport. We left early, planning to stop for dinner in Entebbe on Lake Victoria. I was exhausted and emotionally drained. I was filled with such sadness saying goodbye. America is so far away from Uganda, and my future was still unknown.

Lake Victoria

While we were having dinner, Jonah asked to see my passport. Jonah, who was Collin's older brother, had helped me with passport issues before. When you come into Uganda you request a three-month visa. Mine had expired in December, just before Christmas. At that time, I had gone with another couple I knew to get it renewed at the Ministry of Internal Affairs. After finding the correct line and waiting, I was handed a form with a list of required documents to renew my visa. One document was a letter of reference from an appropriate person stating why I was in-country. This person was my lawyer.

After contacting him and asking for the letter, he stated that he had a friend in the Ministry of Internal Affairs who would meet me and renew my visa. When I showed up, his friend asked if my lawyer had informed me about the money. She demanded $200 dollars. Since my visa expired the next day, this was my lawyer's answer to my request for the required paperwork. I was stuck. I paid.

But you can get only one renewal and, after that, you have to leave the country and re-enter. I had heard that this was simple: take a bus to Kenya, cross the border, and then return. My friends decided to make it a road trip, instead of leaving me to take a bus alone. This worked out well, and I was able to see the landscape in Eastern Uganda, which differed so much from Kampala. Three months later, Jonah took my passport to someone he knew in the Ministry of Internal Affairs and, for a small fee, I got my visa renewed – for the third time.

Then in June, I was invited with a group of friends to go on a bus to Rwanda where they were filming a football tournament. On my return back into Uganda, the Border Agent made a mistake – one which I did not catch.

Now, on the beach in Entebbe, sitting with friends, hours before boarding my flight, Jonah asked to look at my passport and immediately saw the mistake. The Border Agent had stamped my visa (in June) for three days, not three months. I had been living the last three months in Uganda on an expired visa and hadn't known it!

I was in shock and felt sick to my stomach. Matts called a friend who might have answers and Jonah called his friend in the Ministry of Internal Affairs. The answer they got scared me even more. I could try and get on the plane, hoping they would not look too closely at my visa stamp. But if they did, I would be in real trouble. Being in Uganda illegally was a big deal. Most likely I would be detained and then allowed to leave the country after paying a fine of about $5,000, and *banned* from entering Uganda again for three years.

I was in shock. With everything that had happened, this had not even occurred to me. I'd seen the visa stamp and saw the word "three" and didn't understand the shorthand code written next to it that meant three days. I'd assumed it said months. I didn't have money for the fine and I couldn't imagine being banned from this country I loved so much.

After more phone calls, Jonah assured me that his friend could help me fix the problem the next day. I would be able to get a new visa stamp. I had to pay a $300 fee to change my flight to the next day, but this was nothing compared to the $5,000 fine I would have had to pay after being detained.

Emmanuel and I went to the Ministry of Internal Affairs and had no problems getting my visa fixed. Jonah had plans that evening, but we picked up Collins and Matts and, along with Emmanuel, they took me to the airport. As it was, I got into Chicago the day of my brother's wedding and by the time I arrived, I had missed his wedding by about two hours. But my brother and his wife are amazing, and completely understood.

On the long flight home, I thought about all the friends and family that I had left behind. I have such respect for Jack and Connie and the care they have for the families at the guest house, for the staff that works for them, and for the local community. They have shown me what it looks like to serve God and love His people. All the staff at the guest house have my love and friendship. They looked after me, taught me about Uganda, they laughed with me and shared in my sorrows. They work hard and with such joy. I am blessed by their friendships. I was blessed by Grace's wisdom and friendship – and by her cooking.

All my boda drivers and special hire drivers cared for me and kept me safe. They helped me navigate Kampala and they gave me my freedom. By keeping me safe and advising me, they helped me explore so much of Kampala that I would not have been able to do without them.

Abdul and Isma helped me so much during my most difficult times. I am blessed to know Isma, whose integrity and help were invaluable. I am forever thankful for Abdul. Even though we are the same age, he felt like an older brother, protecting me from such harm. I am continually amazed at his wisdom and skill.

Doreen, Esther, Anne, Sarah and Fatuma all cared for me when I rented my own house. They helped me cook and clean. They are my sisters. I will always be grateful for friends I met through Scripture Union or street kids, including Henry, Charles, Joseph, George, Dale, Rajiib and Grace. They were my dear friends, along with so many others who cared for me and lifted me up.

I was heading home having failed, and I was leaving my support group, the ones who had gotten me through all of this. They knew my kids, they knew my heartaches, and understood my anger. They had helped me stay safe and sane. They had accepted me into their families, invited me into their homes over holidays, taken me along to ceremonies, and let me share in their grief during burials. I am even godmother to one couple's first son. My love for Uganda, for Kampala is all wrapped up in the love for its people. I feel so humbled.

I had come to Uganda a year before, not knowing anyone, but I was leaving my heart in Uganda. I was leaving my friends, my family, and children that I loved.

Chapter 5: Life Goes On

"I have passed through the fire and deep water since we parted.
I have forgotten much that I thought I knew, and
learned again much that I had forgotten."
J.R.R. Tolkein, *The Lord of the Rings*

Two weeks after I arrived home, I had an interview for a part-time job. I wanted to be busy. I wanted to numb the heartache and anger. I started working right away, which helped some. Occasionally, I still wrote in my journal.

October 10, 2015

Arriving home again is bittersweet. I'm living a contradiction. My mind can be in Kampala while the rest of me remains here. People are kind and glad that I am home, but do not really want to discuss what happened. I had been warned by another adopting mother who had spent thirteen months in Uganda away from her family that life back home would be a challenge. She said, "Life will have moved on without you and you will have to find where you fit in again." She and my uncle both warned me that I would not be the same person, but not everyone else will understand that.

My uncle had been in Uganda twice while I was there, and had advised me about dealing with my lawyer, had been with me when I met with Mike Chibita, the Deputy of Public Prosecutions, and had met Paul and Sasha. I think he understood more of the way I was and am feeling. It is a comfort to have someone who sympathizes.

I have found it difficult being back. I think most family members want to put the last five years of disappointment behind them – they want to move on. In a way, I feel like I dreamed it all. I spent twelve months in Africa, but some days it seems it never happened. Those thoughts isolate me.

It's been hard coming home to a house that has two bedrooms set up for a returning family. I spent years decorating and planning the kids' rooms. I made quilts and framed artwork. I have a vintage toy box full of toys, and bookshelves with enough kids' books for a library. I have framed pictures in the house of James and Kira, and Benjamin and Anna. I have clothes in the dresser drawers and clothes hanging in the closets. Little boots and shoes by the door. Everything holds a memory attached to when I bought or acquired them, and a dream of the future.

Since getting back, I've been going through the clothes, pulling out some for friends and family, and readying the rest to sell at a consignment shop. I will give away toys and books as Christmas presents, or donate and sell them. I am keeping a very few things – a small Tom and Jerry shirt, a book, a stuffed animal – things I can't yet part with.

But the dream is over, and it's best to move on, or so it seems. As I write this, I have been home for five weeks, and am staying busy with my new job. And I am adjusting. But there are moments – a stupid commercial about hotels welcoming a family adopting a baby, or a church sign announcing a chili supper adoption fundraiser to "Bring Caleb Home" – and I find myself instantly angry and crying.

It's fury and I don't even know where to direct it. It's frustration and complete heartache. It's a feeling of being denied something and a great loss. I had six children whom I got to know, thinking they were mine. Each case was difficult and painful and, of course, it became clear that those children were never to be mine.

But it's hard to fool my heart into moving on. It's hard to erase those hopes and the silly dreams of bedtime and bath time, of cooking together, of Christmas Eve, of school and vacations to Disney World.

It's hard to remove hopes and dreams. Their ghosts still remain, and it is a loss that many may never understand.

November 5, 2015

I just packed the back of my truck full of kids' clothes, toys and books to sell at a local children's consignment shop. I'm torn between phases of crying and rage. I'm so angry. Angry at myself for being so stupid, buying all these clothes and toys. Stupid for thinking I'd have a little girl or boy to dress and read to, play dolls or Legos with. Sometimes I'm angry and don't even know who to be angry with. It's humiliating, too. I have to take this stuff and sell it. If I have to explain it was from a failed adoption, the clerk will wonder why and ask questions. I still struggle with thinking God just made it clear something was wrong with me. I'm not fit to be a mother. That's what people must see in all this mess. I'm caught between heartbreak, anger and shame. It feels so isolating.

November 7, 2015

I was working out at the gym when suddenly a thought of little Sasha hit me so vividly. I instantly pushed it away from my mind so I wouldn't break down at the gym. But afterwards, on my way to meet Mom and Miriam at Grandpa's house, it came again and I couldn't put it aside. Not knowing where she is or who is caring for her, thinking that she could have been mine, my little girl.... I should be hugging and holding her. It was too much and I couldn't breathe. I started crying so hard.

These moments always hit when I least expect them. It doesn't matter if they were not supposed to be adopted, if corrupt people took advantage of them and of me. It doesn't matter that I did the "right" thing in going to the police and cooperating with an investigation.

My heart still hurts and it will forever feel shame for sending Sasha back, for not being strong enough to care for her. I will always feel weak and selfish. I know that I was not strong enough to look out for her. I despise myself and I'm heartbroken. I know the truth. I did not deserve to be her mother. I carry this every day. I try to push it down and away into the back of my mind. But, occasionally, the thoughts pop up and I can no longer deny the pain. It's overwhelming.

November 11, 2015

So I'm reading my American agency's website on Uganda adoptions. Under the "Program in Uganda," it says that they are no longer accepting new applications. Instead, they are working with in-country partnerships, working with reunification, domestic adoption and foster care with Ugandans.

Hmmm….reunification? After all the talk to me at the time about how they do not do reunification. Either this paragraph on their website is referring to my case with James and Kira and how we worked with an agency to bring them back to their mother, or maybe they have done more reunifications since then?

November 21, 2015

I'm trying to calm down and stop crying so much. I have no one to talk to, so I must write. Two weeks ago, I received a message from Isma saying they were taking the investigation to court on Nov. 12. I got a report from him saying, "The RSA (Resident State Authority) instructed us to go ahead and charge the pastor, probation officer, and social worker, and I wrote for the RSA to go ahead and close the foster care program because it's a threat."

So I've been thinking about this all weekend and how it hasn't alleviated my guilt or anger. Mostly I feel empty. But tonight I was on Facebook and Ruth's (the social worker) name popped up for her birthday. I looked at her profile page and then went on to look at the foster program's page and I was in *shock*.

There are two photos of Sasha showing the top of her head and her face. And it says: "Thank you all for your prayers and support of one of our kids cared for by KCA. Sasha has not been able to walk due to a lot of wounds in her private parts and on the head, but after getting treatment, the wounds started to dry."

I couldn't breathe. I was blinded by tears, and overwhelming and helpless guilt. I don't know what to do. I know without a doubt they are using her and her picture and "wounds" to get support and raise money. Any reputable group would not show a small child, give her name and talk about wounds to her private parts.

Why is she not with her parents? Who is she with and why is she getting sores all over? Am I responsible? Am I guilty? Is this child's suffering my fault? I just don't know what to do.

January 18, 2016

How many times can your heart break? A few weeks ago, Pastor Mark was again using Sasha and, this time, also Paul on his Facebook page to get donations. He says Sasha almost died from malaria and typhoid, but was healed by prayer. Now donations are needed....

I've become so callous that I don't trust Pastor Mark at all. I'm also suspicious, because there has been an American woman on their Facebook page more and more since last summer. She claims she is a medical student in Texas, working to become a doctor so she can be the doctor of this "orphanage."

What orphanage?!! She is also fundraising and constantly asking for donations.

There are pictures of her in Kassanda over Christmas, and she is holding Sasha, saying Sasha is now her daughter. At one point, she is asking for donations of thousands of dollars for a machine that detects how much HIV a child has. Does this exist? She is also asking for money for bunkbeds for the orphanage, as all the poor orphans have to sleep on one bed. There is a staged picture of Sasha and other children all on one bed with their eyes closed. They are being used for lies, for money.

There are pictures of them over Christmas, even of Paul, talking about the "orphan." Paul has two parents and an aunt and a grandfather and a village full of family. Sometimes in the pictures they are wearing the clothes I gave them. Other times they are wearing rags. Usually this is in pictures that are asking for money/donations for something.

I did a little searching on this woman mentioned above and found that she has a few last names, she does live in Texas and at one point worked at a local college, but I cannot find any record of her in medical school. I also contacted another adopting family who had a different experience, but ended up contacting the FBI regarding an American who was involved in a scam in Uganda. They were told that until there were multiple complaints, they could not investigate.

I feel responsible for Sasha and feel helpless. I'm so angry. I am so ashamed that I sent her back to those people.

March 12, 2016

Still nothing has happened with the police or arresting the pastor and social worker or probation officer. The program is still running. I know things work on "African time," but this is frustrating. February was the Ugandan presidential elections, and I knew nothing would happen in January or February, as the police were all involved with that. Elections can be violent and unstable.

I've kept in contact with Isma, and I let him know I will send him money to pay for their travel in going to Kassanda to arrest these people. I've contacted Abdul to see if he knows anything. But Abdul has been sick and I don't want to stress him. I don't want to be pushy, but I feel anxiety and I'm worried that this will always continue. The pastor and others will make more money and keep using all these kids. Nothing will ever happen. It all happened to me for no reason. I feel so trapped and helpless.

June 14, 2016

It's ironic to be myself, yet be surprised by myself. Lately, I thought I was doing well, moving on, but I can still be so overcome by emotions. I'm feeling such anger and have uncontrollable crying. I keep having bad dreams, which are also not helping. Last night I dreamt that I was taking Paul and Sasha home to America and the adoption was almost complete. But as we were getting ready for the airport, someone came and took Paul from me.

At work I was trying to show a co-worker pictures of Paul and Sasha. (I still often refer to them as my kids. Why do I do that?) I got on Facebook to show her pictures from the foster program's site and I was suddenly so angry and had tears streaming down my face. It was embarrassing. I had no intention of being emotional.

Again I see this American woman on the Facebook page is making stupid claims. She is now praising Ruth, the social worker, as being her right hand, helping to save these children. This American is also now calling herself a pastor.

I know Paul has family, and I can't do much for him. I couldn't send him to school or help him financially because I know the family would take the money. But when I think of Sasha, I panic. She can never be adopted because there is a file on court about my application for Legal Guardianship (and I was granted guardianship) and then there is a police investigation. So she will never be adopted, but she will forever be used. She is their pawn.

She is cute and young now, so what happens to her as she gets older? What will they continue to do? How does a child cope with being used her entire childhood? Who will fight for her? This remains on my conscience. I failed her.

I'm tired, I'm stressed. I'm angry. I'm helpless and stuck.

Conclusion

*The Lord is close to the brokenhearted and
saves those who are crushed in spirit.*
Psalm 34:18

*"Leave the broken, irreversible past in God's hands, and
step out into the invincible future with Him."*
~ Oswald Chambers

July 14, 2016

I have been home from Uganda for ten months. I'm calling this entry my "Final Chapter," but I know it is not. I decided even before things fell apart with Paul and Sasha that I wanted to write a book. I wanted to write about adoption and how complicated it is. I think of all the families I know who have adopted children, some who have biological children as well. I love these families. I love seeing their family pictures. Seeing kids who were so lost and alone, often struggling with pain and anger and abandonment, but now adjusting, now being loved, now finding their way in this world with a family surrounding them.

I know it's not easy. I know the happy pictures on Facebook do not show all the struggles, the tantrums, the health issues, the language barriers, the heartache and loss these children are going through. I love that their families have the courage to love and continue being strong through all the pain and exhaustion. I know it's worth it, especially when I hear the joy of each small victory, in each milestone. The adoption process is difficult, but the real work begins when families return home.

I didn't make it that far—and I struggle with that. I don't know why I failed at three attempts with six kids. I don't know why I had to go through this while so many others were successful. I've been told it's because God had a plan, He wanted to use me, He knew I'd see the truth with these six kids, He wanted them reunited.... But it's easy to tell myself that God didn't want me to have any children.

Maybe I'd be a terrible mother, so awful that I should be denied any chance. Why couldn't I reunite four of the kids, but still get to be a mother to the last two? Why did I have to be the one to go through this and not someone else?

I turned forty years old at the beginning of this year. It feels like I lost a decade of my life trying to be a mother. Now I'm lost. I have no career and no children. I isolate myself. I don't want to be self-indulgent and waste time feeling sorry for myself—but it's hard to move on. It's hard to even know where I fit in. It's hard to create new dreams.

I still think of Kampala so much. I love that city. I can close my eyes and walk through my neighborhood, ride a boda into the city, and I can see all the places I loved. It's hard to even explain how much I love Uganda. I love my friends there who accepted me with all my faults and welcomed me into their families.

I think of James, and that last day I saw him. I remember hugging him so tightly, both of us crying, and my trying to explain to him that I loved him so much. I'm so thankful for the pictures I've received of James and Kira reunited with their mother in their new home. But I still miss him. I can laugh over memories now of Benjamin and Anna, and how I thought Benjamin would never make it out alive. I think of Anna's smile and I wonder how difficult her life is now, taking care of her brothers.

I think a lot about Paul and wonder if he understands any of this. He was used by adults, even his family, to make money. I wonder if he understands why I sent him back, and worry about the lies they might be telling him, the blame they might place on him. I recall the day I took Paul on a boda into Kampala and we went to Café Java where he had strawberry ice cream for the first time. He was wearing the blue shorts and plaid shirt I bought him. He looked so grown up. Oh, please God, protect his heart. He is still such a little boy.

Thinking of Sasha brings me the most pain. I worry about her every day. I still wish I could find a way to adopt her. I was told by the police that her parents are "up and down," meaning they don't stick around. I think of those few instances when she was happy and I saw her personality – her sense of humor, her silliness, her intelligence. I saw glimpses of the little girl she would be if she had not been hurt and abandoned and used.

I know that Sasha is being used. She is considered a great beauty by Ugandan standards. Even for a three-year-old child. I heard a man in his thirties say he would wait until she was old enough to marry because she was so beautiful. And I know this is why the foster program continues to use her picture when they ask for donations. I worry what will happen to Sasha as she gets older. I worry about her heart, and how she will ever be able to trust anyone. I feel helpless and guilty. I feel unworthy to be her mother. I was just another person who abandoned her.

What I do know is that God can resolve all of this. I know He loves these kids and these families even more than I love them. I know He can take something broken and heal it. I know it's not up to me. Yet I still carry guilt and shame and the pain of failing these kids—and losing my chance to be a mother. Even now I still hope there is a way I can go back for Sasha. It seems improbable and impossible for so many reasons. But I don't know how to put that thought aside.

My editor and I discussed why I wrote this book. We talked about the need for me to share my experiences and to get them down on paper as a caution to future adopting families. But I don't want this book to sound like a therapy session. That seems much too shallow and self-indulgent. My point, simply put, is to hold people accountable. As Christians, we are called to do good works but, too often in adoption, Americans want to adopt for the wrong reasons. We feel we know what defines a good parent. We feel our education and/or our wealth enables us to be a better parent than a mother or father living in poverty.

I met many amazing hardworking Ugandan men and women who try so hard to create better lives for their children. I met families struggling in the slums, and I became friends with women who worked long hours for little pay so they could send their kids to better schools.

They were good parents, the best parents. My life is easier, more privileged, but that would not make me a better parent.

Too often, we are naïve, trusting agencies and lawyers to guide us in a process that is complicated and that we know little about. But we must be accountable to find the truth. It's my responsibility, even when I'm being lied to. I'm responsible to find the truth.

I still see the good that comes from adoption and firmly believe that every child needs a family. But whenever there is poverty and vulnerability, there will be corruption. I never imagined I'd be involved with human traffickers, but in one year (without my knowledge) it happened multiple times.

As an alternative to adopting a child, I feel we need to be more open to adopting families. We may not get to bring a child home, but we can look for opportunities to "adopt" a mother, help her gain sustainability, help her afford to send her children to better schools, to feed and clothe her children. I know that there will always be corruption, and wading through it to find the truth is tiresome and painful. But I think of the joy in those pictures when James and Kira were reunited with their mom. I think of Leah's story of fasting three weeks crying out to God to find Benjamin and Anna. Are there other mothers searching, crying to God for someone to return their children?

And so, I am resigned that my life cannot be the same. I can't go back to who I was – and I don't know the future. I feel a little wiser, a lot older. I feel lost. Even now, I have so much anger and heartache. But I am also so blessed. I am thankful for God's protection and guidance. I'm thankful He used me to reunite those families. I'm so thankful for my family here who loved and supported me. I'm so thankful for all my friends who live here or in Uganda. I'm thankful for those six kids who will always have a place in my heart.

I'm also thankful that this is not the "final chapter." I know I will get back to Uganda. I look forward to that. In the meantime, I will keep trying to heal and find my way.

> *... the Lord delights in those who fear him, who*
> *put their hope in his unfailing love.*
> Psalm 147:11

Printed in the United States
By Bookmasters